Hymns of the Samavedat

Forgotten Books takes the uppermost care to preserve the wording and images from the original book. However, this book has been scanned and reformatted from the original, and as such we cannot guarantee that it is free from errors or contains the full content of the original.

Hymns of the Samavedat

Translated from the Sanskrit by

Ralph T.H. Griffith

First published 1895

Republished 2008 by Forgotten Books

www.forgottenbooks.org

PUBLISHER'S PREFACE

About the Book

"The Sama Veda is a collection of hymns used by the priests during the Soma sacrifice. Many of these duplicate in part or in whole hymns from the Rig Veda. This is a complete translation."

(Quote from sacred-texts.com)

CONTENTS

PREFACE

THE Samaveda, or Veda of Holy Songs, third in the usual order of enumeration of the three Vedas, ranks next in sanctity and liturgical importance to the Rgveda or Veda of Recited praise. Its Sanhita, or metrical portion, consists chiefly of hymns to be chanted by the Udgatar priests at the performance of those important sacrifices in which the juice of the Soma plant, clarified and mixed with milk and other ingredients, was offered in libation to various deities. The Collection is made up of hymns, portions of hymns, and detached verses, taken mainly from the Rgveda, transposed and re-arranged, without reference to their original order, to suit the religious ceremonies in which they were to be employed. In these compiled hymns there are frequent variations, of more or less importance, from the text of the Rgveda as we now possess it which variations, although in some cases they are apparently explanatory, seem in others to be older and more original than the readings of the Rgveda. In singing, the verses are still further altered by prolongation, repetition and insertion of syllables, and various modulations, rests, and other modifications prescribed, for the guidance of the officiating priests, in the Ganas or Song-books. Two of these manuals, the Gramageyagdna, or Congregational, and the Aranyagana or Forest Song-Book, follow the order of the verses of part I, of the Sanhita, and two others, the Uhagana, the Uhyagana, of Part II. This part is less disjointed than part I, and is generally arranged in triplets whose first verse is often the repetition of a verse that has occurred in part I.

There is no clue to the date of the compilation of the Samaveda Hymns, nor has the compiler's name been handed down to us. Such a manual was unnecessary in the early times when the Aryans first came into India, but was required for guidance and use in the complicated ritual elaborated by the invaders after their expansion and settlement in their new homes.

There are three recensions of the text of the Samaveda Sanhita, the Kauthuma Sakha or recension is current in Guzerat, the Jaiminiya in the Carnatic, and the Ranayaniya in the Mahratta country. A translation, by Dr.

Stevenson, of the Ranayaniya recension-or, rather, a free version of Sayana's paraphrase-was edited by Professor Wilson, in 1842; in 1848 Professor Benfey of Göttingen brought out an excellent edition of the same text with a metrical translation, a complete glossary, and explanatory notes; and in 1874-78 Pandit Satyavrata Samasrami of Calcutta published in the Bibliotheca Indicaa. most meritorious edition of the Sanhita according to the same recension, with Sayana's commentary, portions of the Song-books, andi other illustrative matter. I have followed Benfey's text, and have, made much use of his glossary and notes. Pandit Satyavrata Samasrami's edition also has been of the greatest service to me. To Mr. Venis, Principal of the Benares Sanskrit College, I am indebted for, the loan of the College manuscripts of the text and commentary.

I repeat the expression of my obligations to those scholars whose works assisted me in my translation of the Hymns of the Rgveda. For help in translating the non-Rgvedic Hymns of the Samaveda, I am additionally indebted to the late Professor Benfey and to Professor Ludwig whose version will be found in his Der Rgveda, vol. III, pp. 19-25.

For further information regarding the Samaveda Weber's History Of Indian Literature, and Max Müller's History of Ancient Sanskrit Literature, or the article on the Veda in Chamber's Encyclopaedia should be consulted.

R.T.H. GRIFFITH

Kotagiri, Nilgiri
5th May,1893.

FIRST PART

BOOK I.

CHAPTER I.

Om. Glory to the Samaveda! To Lord Ganesa glory! Om.

DECADE I Agni

1. Come, Agni, praised with song, to feast and sacrificial offering: sit
As Hotar on the holy grass!

2. O Agni, thou hast been ordained Hotar of every sacrifice,
By Gods, among the race of men.

3. Agni we choose as envoy, skilled performer of this holy rite,
Hotar, possessor of all wealth.

4. Served with oblation, kindled, bright, through love of song may Agni, bent
On riches, smite the Vritras dead!

5. I laud your most beloved guest like a dear friend, O Agni, him
Who, like a chariot, wins us wealth.

6. Do thou, O Agni, with great might guard us from all malignity,
Yea, from the hate of mortal man!

7. O Agni, come; far other songs of praise will I sing forth to thee.
Wax mighty with these Soma-drops!

8. May Vatsa draw thy mind away even from thy loftiest dwelling place!
Agni, I yearn for thee with song.

9. Agni, Atharvan brought thee forth by rubbing from the sky, the head

Of all who offer sacrifice.

10. O Agni, bring us radiant light to be our mighty succour, for
Thou art our visible deity!

DECADE II Agni

1. O Agni, God, the people sing reverent praise to thee for strength:
With terrors trouble thou the foe

2. I seek with song your messenger, oblation-bearer, lord of wealth,
Immortal, best at sacrifice.

3. Still turning to their aim in thee the sacrificer's sister hymns
Have come to thee before the wind.

4. To thee, illuminer of night, O Agni, day by day with prayer,
Bringing thee reverence, we come.

5. Help, thou who knowest lauds, this work, a lovely hymn in Rudra's praise,
Adorable in every house!

6. To this fair sacrifice to drink the milky draught art thou called forth:
O Agni, with the Maruts come!

7. With homage will I reverence thee, Agni, like a long-tailed steed,
Imperial lord of holy rites.

8. As Aurva and as Bhrigu called, as Apnavana called, I call
The radiant Agni robed with sea.

9. When he enkindles Agni, man should with his heart attend the song:
I kindle Agni till he glows.

10. Then, verily, they see the light refulgent of primeval seed,
Kindled on yonder side of heaven.

DECADE III Agni

1. Hither, for powerful kinship, I call Agni, him who prospers you,
Most frequent at our solemn rites.

2. May Agni with his pointed blaze cast down each fierce devouring fiend:
May Agni win us wealth by war!

3. Agni, be gracious; thou art great: thou hast approached the pious man,
Hast come to sit on sacred grass.

4. Agni, preserve us, from distress consume our enemies, O God,
Eternal, with thy hottest flames

5. Harness, O Agni, O thou God, thy steeds which are most excellent!
The fleet ones bring thee rapidly.

6. Lord of the tribes, whom all must seek, we worshipped Agni set thee down,
Refulgent, rich in valiant men.

7. Agni is head and height of heaven, the master of the earth is he
He quickeneth the waters' seed.

8. O Agni, graciously announce this our good fortune of the Gods,
And this our newest hymn of praise!

9. By song, O Agni, Angiras! Gopavana hath brought thee forth
Hear thou my call, refulgent one!

10. Agni, the Sage, the Lord of Strength, hath moved around the sacred gifts,

Giving the offerer precious things.

11. His heralds bear him up aloft, the God who knoweth all that lives,
The Sun, that all may look on him.

12. Praise Agni in the sacrifice, the Sage whose holy laws are true
The God who driveth grief away.

13. Kind be the Goddesses to lend us help, and kind that we may drink:
May their streams bring us health and wealth

14. Lord of the brave, whose songs dost thou in thine abundance now inspire,
Thou whose hymns help to win the kine?

DECADE IV Agni

1. Sing to your Agni with each song, at every sacrifice for strength.
Come, let us praise the wise and, everlasting God even as a well-beloved friend,

2. Agni, protect thou us by one, protect us by the second song,
Protect us by three hymns, O Lord of power and might, bright God, by four hymns guard us well!

3. O Agni, with thy lofty beams, with thy pure brilliancy, O God,
Kindled, most youthful one! by Bharadvaja's hand, shine on us richly, holy Lord!

4. O Agni who art worshipped well, dear let our princes be to thee,
Our wealthy patrons who are governors of men, who part, as gifts, the stall of kine!

Agni, praise-singer! Lord of men, God! burning up the Rakshasas,

5. Mighty art thou, the ever-present, household-lord! home-friend and guardian from the sky.

6. Immortal Jatavedas, thou bright-hued refulgent gift of Dawn,
Agni, this day to him who pays oblations bring the Gods who waken with the morn!

7. Wonderful, with thy favouring help, send us thy bounties, gracious Lord.
Thou art the charioteer, Agni, of earthly wealth: find rest and safety for our seed!

8. Famed art thou, Agni, far and wide, preserver, righteous, and a Sage.
The holy singers, O enkindled radiant one, ordainers, call on thee to come.

9. O holy Agni, give us wealth famed among men and strengthening life!
Bestow on us, O helper, that which many crave, more glorious still through righteousness!

10. To him, who dealeth out all wealth, the sweet-toned Hotar-priest of men,
To him like the first vessels filled with savoury juice, to Agni let the lauds go forth.

DECADE V Agni

1. With this mine homage I invoke Agni for you, the Son of Strength,
Dear, wisest envoy, skilled in noble sacrifice, immortal messenger of all.

2. Thou liest in the logs that are thy mothers: mortals kindle thee.
Alert thou bearest off the sacrifieer's gift, and then thou shinest to the Gods.

3. He hath appeared, best prosperer, in whom men lay their holy acts:
So may our songs of praise come nigh to Agni who was born to give the Arya strength!

4. Chief Priest is Agni at the laud, as stones and grass at sacrifice.
Gods! Maruts! Brahmanaspati! I crave with song the help that is most excellent.

5. Pray Agni of the piercing flame, with sacred songs, to be our help;
For wealth, famed Agni, Purumilha and ye men! He is Suditi's sure defence.

6. Hear, Agni who hast ears to hear, with all thy train of escort Gods!
With those who come at dawn let Mitra, Aryaman sit on the grass at sacrifice.

7. Agni of Divodasa, God, comes forth like Indra in his might.
Rapidly hath he moved along his mother earth: he stands in high heaven's dwelling-place.

8. Whether thou come from earth or from the lofty lucid realm of heaven,
Wax stronger in thy body through my song of praise: fill full all creatures, O most wise!

9. If, loving well the forests, thou wentest to thy maternal floods,
Not to be scorned, Agni, is that return of thine when, from afar, thou now art here.

10. O Agni, Manu stablished thee a light for all the race of men:
With Kanva hast thou blazed, Law-born and waxen strong, thou whom the people reverence.

CHAPTER II.

DECADE I Agni

1. The God who giveth wealth accept your full libation poured to, him!
Pour ye it out, then fill the vessel full again, for so the God regardeth you.

2. Let Brahmanaspati come forth, let Sunrita the Goddess come,
And Gods bring to our rite which yields a fivefold gift the hero, lover of mankınd!

3. Stand up erect to lend us aid, stand up like Savitar the God,
Erect as strength-bestower when we call on thee with priests who balm our offerings!

4. The man who bringeth gifts to thee, bright God who fain wouldst lead to wealth,
Winneth himself a brave son, Agni! skilled in lauds, one prospering in a thousand ways.

5. With hymns and holy eulogies we supplicate your Agni, Lord
Of many families who duly serve the Gods, yea, him whom others too inflame.

6. This Agni is the Lord of great prosperity and hero, strength,
Of wealth with noble offspring and with store of kine, the Lord of battles with the foe.

7. Thou, Agni, art the homestead's Lord, our Hotar-priest at sacrifice.
Lord of all boons, thou art the Potar, passing wise. Pay worship, and enjoy the good!

8. We as thy friends have chosen thee, mortals a God, to be our help.
The Waters' Child, the blessed, the most mighty one, swift conqueror, and without a peer.

DECADE II Agni

1. Present oblations, make him splendid: set ye as Hotar in his place the Home's Lord, worshipped
With gifts and homage where they pour libations! Honour him meet for reverence in our houses.

2. Verily wondrous is the tender youngling's growth who never draweth nigh to drink his mother's milk.
As soon as she who hath no udder bore him, he, faring on his. great errand, suddenly grew strong.

3. Here is one light for thee, another yonder: enter the third and, be therewith united.
Beautiful be thy union with the body, beloved in the Gods' sublimest birthplace!

4. For Jatavedas, worthy of our praise, will we frame with our mind this eulogy as 'twere a car;
For good, in his assembly, is this care of ours. Let us not, in thy friendship, Agni, suffer harm!

5. Agni Vaisvanara, born in course of Order, the messenger of earth, the head of heaven,
The Sage, the sovran, guest of men, our vessel fit for their mouth, the Gods have generated.

6. Even as the waters from the mountain ridges, so sprang the; Gods, through lauds, from thee, O Agni.
To thee speed hymns and eulogies, as horses haste, bearing him who loves the song, to battle.

7. Win to protect you, Rudra, lord of worship, priest of both worlds, effectual sacrificer,
Agni, invested with his golden colours, before the thunder strike and lay you senseless!

8. The King whose face is decked with oil is kindled with homage offered by his faithful servant.
The men, the priests adore him with oblations. Agni hath shone forth at the flush of morning.

9. Agni advanceth with his lofty banner: through earth and heaven the Bull hath loudly bellowed
He hath come nigh from the sky's farthest limit: the Steer hath waxen in the waters' bosom.

10. From the two fire-sticks have the men engendered with thoughts, urged by the hand, the glorious Agni,
Far-seen, with pointed flame, Lord of the Homestead.

DECADE III Agni

1. Agni is wakened by the people's fuel to meet the Dawn who cometh like a milch-cow.
Like young trees shooting up on high their branches, his flames. are mounting to the vault of heaven.

2. Set forth the gleaming one, the song-inspirer, not foolish with. the foolish, fort-destroyer,
Who leadeth with his hymns to thought of conquest, gold-bearded, richly splendid with his armour

3. Thou art like heaven: one form is bright, one holy, like Day and Night dissimilar in colour.

All magic powers thou aidest, self-dependent! Auspicious bethy bounty here, O Pushan!

4. As holy food, Agni, to thine invoker give wealth in cattle, lasting, rich in marvels!
To us be born a son and spreading offspring. Agni, be this thy gracious will to us-ward!

5. Stablished to fill the juice with vital vigour, giver of wealth, guard of his servant's body,
The great Priest, born, who knows the clouds, abider with men, is seated in the waters' eddy.

6. Let the song, honouring the best, with longing honour the Asura's most famous sovran,
The deeds of him the mighty, deeds like Indra's, the manly one in whom the folk must triumph!

7. In the two kindling-blocks lies Jatavedas like the well-cherished germ in pregnant women,--
Agni who day by day must be entreated by men who watch provided with oblations.

8. Agni, from days of old thou slayest demons: never shall Rakshasas in fight o'ercome thee.
Burn up the foolish ones, raw flesh devourers: let none of them escape thine heavenly arrow!

DECADE IV Agni

1. Bring us most mighty splendour thou, Agni, resistless on thy way:
Prepare for us the path that leads to glorious opulence and strength!

2. May the brave man, if full of zeal he serve and kindle Agni's flame,
Duly presenting sacred gifts, enjoy the Gods' protecting help.

3. Thy bright smoke lifts itself aloft, and far-extended shines in heaven,
For, Purifier! like the Sun thou beamest with thy radiant glow.

4. Thou, Agni, even as Mitra, hast a princely glory of thine own.
Bright, active God, thou makest fame increase like means of nourishment.

5. At dawn let Agni, much-beloved, guest of the house, be glorified,
In whom, the everlasting one, all mortals make their offerings blaze.

6. Most moving song be Agni's: shine on high, O rich in radiant light!
Like the chief consort of a King riches and strength proceed from thee.

7. Exerting all our strength with thoughts of power we glorify in speech
Agni your dear familiar friend, the darling guest in every house.

8. His beam hath lofty power of life: sing praise to Agni, to the God
Whom men have set in foremost place, like Mitra for their eulogy!

9. To noblest Agni, friend of man, chief Vritra-slayer, have we come-
Who with Srutarvan, Riksha's son, in lofty presence is inflamed.

10. Born as the loftiest Law commands, comrade of those who grew with him.
Agni, the sire of Kasyapa by faith, the mother, Manu, Sage.

DECADE V Agni

1. We in King Soma place our trust, in Agni, and in Varuna,
The Aditya, Vishnu, Surya, and the Brahman-priest Brihaspati.

2. Hence have these men gone up on high and mounted to the heights of heaven:
On! conquer on the path by which Angirasas travelled to the skies!

3. That thou mayst send us ample wealth, O Agni, we will kindler thee:
So, for the great oblation, Steer, pray Heaven and Earth to come to us!

4. He runs when one calls after him, This is the prayer of him who prays.
He holds all knowledge in his grasp even as the felly rounds the wheel.

5. Shoot forth, O Agni, with thy flame: demolish them on every side!
Break down the Yatudhana's strength, the vigour of the Rakshasa!

6. Worship the Vasus, Agni! here, the Rudras and Adityas, all
Who know fair sacrifices, sprung from Mann, scattering blessings down!

BOOK II.

CHAPTER I.

DECADE I Agni

1. Agni, thy faithful servant I call upon thee with many a gift,
As in the keeping of the great inciting God.

2. To Agni, to the Hotar-priest offer your best, your lofty speech,
To him ordainer-like who bears the light of songs.

3. O Agni, thou who art the lord of wealth in kine, thou Son of Strength,
Bestow on us, O Jatavedas, high renown

4. Most skilled in sacrifice, bring the Gods, O Agni, to the pious, man:
A joyful Priest, thy splendour drives our foes afar

5. Taught by seven mothers at his birth was he, for glory of the wise.
He, firm and sure, hath set his mind on glorious wealth

6. And in the day our prayer is this: May Aditi come nigh to help,
With loving-kindness bring us weal and chase our foes

7. Worship thou Jatavedas, pray to him who willingly accepts,
Whose smoke wanders at will, and none may grasp his flame

8. No mortal man can e'er prevail by arts of magic over him
Who hath served Agni well, the oblation-giving God.

9. Agni, drive thou the wicked foe, the evil-hearted thief away,
Far, far, Lord of the brave! and give us easy paths!

10. O hero Agni, Lord of men, on hearing this new laud of mine

Burn down the Rakshasas, enchanters, with thy flame!

DECADE II Agni

1. Sing forth to him the holy, most munificent, sublime with his refulgent glow,
To Agni, ye Upastutas

2. Agni, he conquers by thine aid that brings him store of valiant sons and does great deeds,
Whose bond of friendship is thy choice

3. Sing praise to him the Lord of light! The Gods have made the God to be their messenger,
To bear oblation to the Gods.

4. Anger not him who is our guest! He is the bright God Agni, praised by many a man,
God Hotar, skilled in sacrifice.

5. May Agni, worshipped, bring us bliss: may the gift, blessed one! and sacrifice bring bliss.
Yea, may our eulogies bring bliss.

6. Thee have we chosen skilfullest in sacrifice, immortal Priest among the Gods,
Wise finisher of this holy rite.

7. Bring us that splendour, Agni, which may overcome each greedy fiend in our abode,
And the malicious wrath of men!

8. Soon as the eager Lord of men is friendly unto Manu's race
Agni averteth from us all the Rakshasas!

DECADE III Indra

1. Sing this, beside the flowing juice, to him your hero, much-invoked,
To please him as a mighty Bull

2. O Satakratu Indra, now rejoice with that carouse of thine
Which is most glorious of all!

3. Ye cows, protect the fount: the two mighty ones bless the sacrifice.
The handles twain are wrought of gold.

4. Sing praises that the horse may come; sing, Srutakaksha, that the cow
May come, that Indra's might may come

5. We make this Indra very strong to strike, the mighty Vritra dead:
A vigorous hero shall he be.

6. Based upon strength and victory and power, O Indra, is thy birth:
Thou, mighty one! art strong indeed,

7. The sacrifice made Indra great when he unrolled the earth, and made
Himself a diadem in heaven.

8. If I, O Indra, were, like thee, the single ruler over wealth
My worshipper should be rich in kine.

9. Pressers, blend Soma juice for him, each draught most excellent, for him
The brave, the hero, for his joy.

10. Here is the Soma juice expressed. O Vasu, drink till thou art full:
Undaunted God, we give it thee

DECADE IV Indra

1. Surya, thou mountest up to meet the hero famous for his wealth,

Who hurls the bolt and works for man.

2. Whatever, Vritra-slayer! thou, Surya hast risen upon to-day,
That, Indra, all is in thy power.

3. That Indra is our youthful friend, who with his trusty guidanceled
Turvasa, Yadu from afar.

4. O Indra, let not ill designs surround us in the sunbeams' light
This may we gain with thee for friend!

5. Indra, bring wealth that gives delight, the victor's ever-conquering
wealth,
Most excellent, to be our aid

6. In mighty battle we invoke Indra, Indra is lesser fight,
The friend who bends his bolt at fiends.

7. In battle of a thousand arms Indra drank Kadru's Soma juice
There he displayed his manly might.

8. Faithful to thee, we sing aloud, heroic Indra, songs to thee
Mark, O good Lord, this act of ours!

9. Hitherward! they who light the flame and straightway trim the sacred
grass,
Whose friend is Indra ever young.

10. Drive all our enemies away, smite down the foes who press around,
And bring the wealth for which we long!

DECADE V Indra and others

1. I Hear, as though 'twere close at hand, the cracking of the whips they
hold:

They gather splendour on their way.

2. Indra, these friends of ours, supplied with Soma, wait and look to thee
As men with fodder to the herd.

3. Before his hot displeasure all the peoples, all the men bow down,
As rivers bow them to the sea.

4. We choose unto ourselves that high protection of the mighty Gods,
That it may help and succour us.

5. O Brahmanaspati, make thou Kakshivan Ausija a loud
Chanter of flowing Soma juice!

6. Much honoured with libations may the Vritra-slayer watch for us:
May Sakra listen to our prayer

7. Send us this day, God Savitar, prosperity with progeny
Drive thou the evil dream away!

8. Where is that ever-youthful Steer, strong-necked and never yet bent down?
What Brahman ministers to him?

9. There where the mountains downward slope, there at the meeting of the streams
The Sage was manifest by song.

10. Praise Indra whom our songs must laud, sole sovran of mankind, the chief
Most liberal who controlleth men

CHAPTER II.

DECADE I Indra and others

1. Indra whose jaws are strong hath drunk of worshipping Sudaksha's draught,
The Soma juice with barley brew.

2. O Lord of ample wealth, these songs of praise have called aloud to thee,
Like milch-kine lowing to their calves!

3. Then straight they recognized the mystic name of the creative Steer,
There in the mansion of the Moon.

4. When Indra, strongest hero, brought the streams, the mighty waters down,
Pushan was standing by his side.

5. The Cow, the streaming mother of the liberal Maruts, pours her milk,
Harnessed to draw their chariots on.

6. Come, Lord of rapturous joys, to our libation with thy bay steeds, come
With bay steeds to the flowing juice

7. Presented strengthening gifts have sent Indra away at sacrifice,
With night, unto the cleansing bath.

8. I from my Father have received deep knowledge of eternal Law:
I was born like unto the Sun.

9. With Indra splendid feasts be ours, rich in all strengthening things,
wherewith,

Wealthy in food, we may rejoice

10. Soma and Pushan, kind to him who travels to the Gods, provide
Dwellings all happy and secure.

DECADE II Indra

1. Invite ye Indra with a song to drink your draught of Soma steeds, juice,
All-conquering Satakratu, most munificent of all who live

2. Sing ye a song, to make him glad, to Indra, Lord of tawny
The Soma-drinker, O my friends!

3. This, even this, O Indra, we implore: as thy devoted friends
The Kanvas praise thee with their hymns!

4. For Indra, lover of carouse, loud be our songs about the juice
Let poets sing the song of praise.

5. Here, Indra, is thy Soma draught, made pure upon the sacred grass:
Run hither, come and drink thereof

6. As a good cow to him who milks, we call the doer of good deeds
To our assistance duy by day.

7. Hero, the Soma being shed, I pour the juice for thee to drink
Sate thee and finish thy carouse!

8. The Soma, Indra, which is shed in saucers and in cups for thee,
Drink thou, for thou art lord thereof!

9. In every need, in every fray we call, as friends, to succour us,
Indra, the mightiest of all.

10. O come ye hither, sit ye down: to Indra sing ye forth your song,

Companions, bringing hymns of praise

DECADE III Indra

1. So, Lord of affluent gifts, this juice hath been expressed for thee with strength:
Drink of it, thou who lovest song!

2. Great is our Indra from of old; greatness be his, the Thunderer
Wide as the heaven extends his might.

3. Indra, as one with mighty arm, gather for us with thy right hand
Manifold and nutritious spoil!

4. Praise, even as he is known, with song Indra the guardian of the kine,
The Son of Truth, Lord of the brave.

5. With what help will he come to us, wonderful, ever-waxing friend?
With what most mighty company?

6. Thou speedest down to succour us this ever-conquering God of yours
Him who is drawn to all our songs.

7. To the assembly's wondrous Lord, the lovely friend of Indra, I
Had prayed for wisdom and successs.

8. May all thy paths beneath the sky whereby thou speddest Vyasva on,
Yea, let all spaces hear our voice

9. Bring to us all things excellent, O Satakratu, food and strength,
For, Indra, thou art kind to us!

10. Here is the Soma ready pressed: of this the Maruts, yea, of this,
Self-luminous the Asvins drink.

DECADE IV Indra and others

1. Tossing about, the active ones came nigh to Indra at his birth,
Winning themselves heroic might.

2. Never, O Gods, do we offend, nor are we ever obstinate
We walk as holy texts command.

3. Evening is come: sing loudly thou Atharvan's nobly singing son:
Give praise to Savitar the God!

4. Now Morning with her earliest light shines forth, dear daughter of the Sky:
High, Asvins, I extol your praise.

5. Armed with the bones of dead Dadhyach, Indra, with unresisted might
The nine-and-ninety Vritras slew.

6. Come, Indra, and delight thee with the juice at all our Soma feasts,
Protector, mighty in thy strength

7. O thou who slayest Vritras, come, O Indra, hither to our side,
Mighty one, with thy mighty aids!

8. That might of his shone brightly forth when Indra brought together, like
A skin, the worlds of heaven and earth,

9. This is thine own Thou drawest near, as turns a pigeon to his mate:
Thou carest, too, for this our prayer.

10. May Vata breathe his balm on us, healthful, delightful to our heart:
May he prolong our days of life

DECADE V Indra and others

1. Ne'er is he injured whom the Gods Varuna, Mitra, Aryam.
The excellently wise, protect.

2. According to our wish for kine, for steeds and chariots, as of old,
Be gracious to our wealthy chiefs

3. Indra, these spotted cows yield thee their butter and the milky draught,
Aiders, thereby, of sacrifice.

4. That thou much-lauded! many-named! mayst, with this thought, that longs for milk,
Come to each Soma sacrifice.

5. May bright Sarasvati, endowed with plenteous wealth and spoil, enriched
With prayer, desire the sacrifice.

6. Why 'mid the Nahusha tribes shall sate this Indra with his Soma juice?
He shall bring precious things to us.

7. Come, we have pressed the juice for thee; O Indra, drink this Soma here:
Sit thou on this my sacred grass

8. Great, unassailable must be the heavenly favour of the Three,
Varuna, Mitra, Aryaman.

9. We, Indra, Lord of ample wealth, our guide, depend on one like thee,
Thou driver of the tawny steeds!

BOOK III.

CHAPTER I.

DECADE I Indra

1. Let Soma juices make thee glad! Display thy bounty, Thunderer:
Drive off the enemies of prayer!

2. Drink our libation, Lord of hymns! with streams of meath thou art
bedewed:
Yea, Indra, glory Is thy gift.

3. Indra hath ever thought of you and tended you with care. The God,
Heroic Indra, is not checked.

4. Let the drops pass within thee as the rivers flow into the sea
O Indra, naught excelleth thee!

5. Indra, the singers with high praise, Indra reciters with their lauds,
Indra the choirs have glorified.

6. May Indra give, to aid us wealth handy that rules the skilful ones!
Yea, may the Strong give potent wealth

7. Verily Indra, conquering all, drives even mighty fear away,
For firm is he and swift to act.

8. These songs with every draught we pour come, lover of the song, to thee
As milch-kine hasten to their calves.

9. Indra and Wishan will we call for friendship and prosperity,
And for the winning of the spoil.

10. O Indra, Vritra-slayer, naught is better, mightier than thou
Verily there is none like thee!

DECADE II Indra

1. Him have I magnified, our Lord in common, guardian of your folk,
Discloser of great wealth in kine.

2. Songs have outpoured themselves to thee, Indra, the strong, the guardian Lord,
And with one will have risen to thee!

3. Good guidance hath the mortal man whom Arya-man, the Marut host,
And Mitras, void of guile, protect.

4. Bring us the wealth for which we long, O Indra, that which is concealed
In strong firm place precipitous.

5. Him your best Vritra-slayer, him the famous champion of mankind
I urge to great munificence.

6. Indra, may we adorn thy fame, fame of one like thee, hero! deck,
Sakra! thy fame at highest feast!

7. Indra, accept at break of day our Soma mixt with roasted corn,
With groats, with cake, with eulogies!

8. With waters' foam thou torest off, Indra, the head of Namuchi,
When thou o'ercamest all the foes.

9. Thine are these Soma juices, thine, Indra, those still to be expressed:
Enjoy them, Lord of princely wealth!

10. For thee, O Indra, Lord of light, Somas are pressed and grass is strewn:
Be gracious to thy worshippers!

1. We seeking strength, with Soma drops fill full your Indra like a well,
Most liberal, Lord of boundless might.

2. O Indra, even from that place come unto us with food that gives
A hundred, yea, a thousand powers!

3. The new-born Vritra-slayer asked his mother, as he seized his shaft,
Who are the, fierce and famous ones?

4. Let us call him to aid whose hands stretch far, the highly-lauded, who
Fulfils the work to favour us

5. Mitra who knoweth leadeth us, and Varuna who guideth straight,
And Aryaman in accord with Gods.

6. When, even as she were present here, red Dawn hath shone from far
away,
She spreadeth light on every side.

7. Varuna, Mitra, sapient pair, pour fatness on our pastures, pour
Meath on the regions of the air!

8. And, at our sacrifices, these, sons, singers, have enlarged their bounds,
So that the cows must walk knee-deep.

9. Through all this world strode Vishnu: thrice his foot he planted, and the
whole
Was gathered in his footstep's dust.

DECADE IV Indra

1. Pass by the wrathful offerer; speed the man who pours libation, drink
The juice which he presents to thee!

2. What is the word addressed to him, God great and excellently wise?
For this is what exalteth him.

3, His wealth who hath no store of kine hath ne'er found out recited laud,
Nor song of praises that is sung.

4. Lord of each thing that giveth strength, Indra delighteth most in lauds,
Borne by bay steeds, libations' friend.

5. With wealth to our libation come, be not thou angry with us, like
A great man with a youthful bride.

6. When, Vasu, wilt thou love the laud? Now let the Channel bring the
stream.
The juice is ready to ferment.

7. After the Seasons. Indra, drink the Soma from the Brahman's gift:
Thy friendship is invincible!
S. O Indra, lover of the song, we are the singers of thy praise
O Soma-drinker, quicken us!

9. O Indra, in each fight and fray give to our bodies manly strength:
Strong Lord, grant ever-conquering might!

10. For so thou art the brave man's friend; a hero, too, art thou, and strong:
So may thine heart be won to us!

DECADE V Indra

1. Like kine unmilked we call aloud, hero, to thee, and sing thy praise,
Looker on heavenly light, Lord of this moving world, Lord, Indra, of what
moveth not!

2. That we may win us wealth and power we poets, verily, call on thee:

In war men call on thee, Indra, the hero's Lord, in the steed's race-course call on thee:

3. To you will I sing Indra's praise who gives good gifts as well we know;
The praise of Maghavan who, rich in treasure, aids his singers with wealth thousandfold.

4. As cows low to their calves in stalls, so with our songs we glorify
This Indra, even your wondrous God who checks attack, who takes delight in precious juice.

5. Loud singing at the sacred rite where Soma flows we priests invoke
With haste, that he may help, as the bard's cherisher, Indra who findeth wealth for you

6. With Plenty for his true ally the active man will gain the spoil.
Your Indra, much invoked, I bend with song, as bends a wright his wheel of solid wood.

7. Drink, Indra, of the savoury juice, and cheer thee with our milky draught!
Be, for our weal, our friend and sharer of the feast, and let thy wisdom guard us well!

8. For thou--come to the worshipper!--wilt find great wealth to make us rich.
Fill thyself full, O Maghavan, for gain of kine, full, Indra, for the gain of steeds!

9. Vasishtha will not overlook the lowliest one among you all
Beside our Soma juice effused to-day let all the Maruts drink with eager haste!

10. Glorify naught besides, O friends; so shall no sorrow trouble you!
Praise only mighty Indra when the juice is shed, and say your lauds repeatedly!

CHAPTER II.

DECADE I Indra

1. No one by deed attains to him who works and strengthens evermore:
No, not by sacrifice, to Indra. praised of all, resistless, daring, bold in might.

2. He without ligature, before making incision in the neck,
Closed up the wound again, most wealthy Maghavan, who healeth the dissevered parts.

3. A thousand and a hundred steeds are harnessed to thy golden car:
Yoked by devotion, Indra, let the long-maned bays bring thee to drink the Soma juice!

4. Come hither, Indra, with bay steeds, joyous, with tails like peacock's plumes!
Let no men check thy course as fowlers stay the bird: pass o'er them as o'er desert lands!

5. Thou as a God, O mightiest, verily blessest mortal man.
O Maghavan, there is no comforter but thou: Indra, I speak my words to thee.

6. O Indra, thou art far-renowned, impetuous Lord of power and might.
Alone, the never-conquered guardian of mankind, thou smitest
down resistless foes.

7. Indra for worship of the Gods, Indra while sacrifice proceeds,
Indra, as warriors in the battle-shock, we call, Indra that we may win the spoil.

8. May these my songs of praise exalt thee, Lord, who hast abundant wealth!
Men skilled in holy hymns, pure, with the hues of fire, have sung them with their lauds to thee.

9. These songs of ours exceeding sweet, these hymns of praise ascend to thee,
Like ever-conquering chariots that display their strength gain wealth and give unfailing help.

10. Even as the wild-bull, when he thirsts, goes to the desert's watery pool,
Come to us quickly both at morning and at eve, and with the Kanvas drink thy fill!

DECADE II Indra and others

1. Indra, with all thy saving helps assist us, Lord of power and might!
For after thee we follow even as glorious bliss, thee, hero, finderout of wealth.

2. O Indra, Lord of light, what joys thou broughtest from the Asuras,
Prosper therewith, O Maghavan, him who lauds that deed, and those whose grass is trimmed for thee!

3. To Aryaman and Mitra sing a reverent song, O pious one,
A pleasant hymn to Varuna who shelters us: sing ye a laud unto the Kings!

4. Men with their lauds are urging thee, Indra, to drink the Soma first.
The Ribhus in accord have lifted up their voice, and Rudras sung thee as the first.

5. Sing to your lofty Indra, sing, Maruts, a holy hymn of praise
Let Satakratu, Vritra-slayer, slay the foe with hundred-knotted thunderbolt!

6. To Indra sing the lofty hymn, Maruts! that slays the Vritras best,

Whereby the holy ones created for the God the light divine that ever wakes.

7. O Indra, give us wisdom as a sire gives wisdom to his sons
Guide us, O much-invoked, in this our way: may we still live and look upon the light!

8. O Indra, turn us not away: be present with us at our feast
For thou art our protection, yea, thou art our kin: O Indra, turn us not away!

9. We compass these like waters, we whose grass is trimmed and Soma pressed.
Here where the filter pours its stream, thy worshippers round
thee, O Vritra-slayer, sit.

10. All strength and valour that is found, Indra, in tribes of Nahushas,
And all the splendid fame that the Five Tribes enjoy, bring, yea, all manly powers at once!

DECADE III Indra

1. Yea, verily thou art a Bull, our guardian, rushing like a bull:
Thou, mighty one, art celebrated as a Bull, famed as a Bull both near and far.

2. Whether, O Sakra, thou be far, or, Vritra-slayer, near at hand,
Thence by heaven-reaching songs he who bath pressed the juice invites thee with thy long-maned steeds.

3. In the wild raptures of the juice sing to your hero with high laud, to him the wise,
To Indra glorious in his name, the mighty one, even as the hymn alloweth it!

4. O Indra, give us for our weal a triple refuge, triply strong!
Bestow a dwelling-place on our rich lords and me, and keep thy dart afar
from these!

5. Turning, as 'twere, to meet the Sun enjoy from Indra all good things!
When he who will be born is born with power we look to treasures as our
heritage.

6. The godless mortal gaineth not this food, O thou whose life is long!
But one who yokes the bright-hued horses, Etasas; then Indra yokes his
tawny steeds.

7. Draw near unto our Indra who must be invoked In every fight!
Come, thou most mighty Vritra-slayer, meet for praise, come to, libations
and to hymns!

8. Thine, Indra, is the lowest wealth, thou cherishest the midmost wealth,
Thou ever rulest all the highest: in the fray for cattle none resisteth thee.

9. Where art thou? Whither art thou gone? For many a place attracts thy
mind.
Haste, warrior, fort-destroyer, Lord of battle's din! haste, holy songs have
sounded forth!

10. Here, verily, yesterday we let the thunder-wielder drink his fill.
Bring him the juice poured forth in sacrifice to-day. Now range you by the
glorious one!

DECADE IV Indra

1. He who as sovran Lord of men moves with his chariots unrestrained,
The Vritra-slayer, vanquisher of fighting hosts, pre-eminent, is praised in
song.

2. Indra, give us security from that whereof we are afraid

Help us, O Maghavan, let thy favour aid us thus; drive away foes and enemies!

3. Strong pillar thou, Lord of the home! armour of Soma-offerers!
The drop of Soma breaketh all the strongholds down, and Indra is the Rishis' friend.

4. Verily, Surya, thou art great; truly, Aditya, thou art great!
O most admired for greatness of thy majesty, God, by thy greatness thou art great!

5. Indra! thy friend, when fair of form and rich in chariots, steeds, and kine,
Hath ever vital power that gives him strength, and joins the company with radiant men.

6. O Indra, if a hundred heavens and if a hundred earths were thine,--
No, not a hundred suns could match thee at thy birth, not both the worlds, O Thunderer!

7. Though, Indra, thou art called by men eastward and west ward, north and south,
Thou chiefly art with Anava and Turvasa, brave champion urged by men to come.

8. Indra whose wealth is in thyself, what mortal will attack this man?
The strong will win the spoil on the decisive day through faith in thee, O Maghavan!

9. First, Indra! Agni! hath this Maid come footless unto those with feet.
Stretching her head and speaking loudly with her tongue, she hath gone downward thirty steps.

10. Come, Indra, very near to us with aids of firmly-based resolve
Come, most auspicious, with thy most auspicious help; good kinsman, with good kinsmen come!

DECADE V Indra.

1. Call to your aid the eternal one who shoots and none may shoot at him,
Inciter, swift, victorious, best of charioteers, unconquered, Tugriya's strengthener!

2. Let none, no, not thy worshippers, delay thee far away from us
Even from faraway come thou unto our feast, or listen if' already here!

3. For Indra Soma-drinker, armed with thunder, press the Soma juice;
Make ready your dressed meats: cause him to favour us! The giver blesses him who gives.

4. We call upon that Indra who, most active, ever slays the foe
With boundless spirit, Lord of heroes, manliest one, help thou and prosper us in fight!

5. Ye rich in strength, through your great power vouchsafe us blessings day and night!
The offerings which we bring to you shall never fail gifts brought by us shall never fail.

6. Whenever mortal worshipper will sing a bounteous giver's praise,
Let him with song inspired laud Varuna who supports the folk who follow varied rites.

7. Drink milk to Indra in the joy of Soma juice, Medhyatithi!
To golden Indra ever close to his bay steeds, the thunder-armed, the golden one!

8. Both boons,-may Indra, hitherward turned listen to this prayer of ours,
And mightiest Maghavar, with thought inclined to us come near to drink the Soma juice!

9. Not for an ample price dost thou, Stone-caster! give thyself away,
Not for a thousand, Thunderer! nor ten thousand, nor a hundred, Lord of countless wealth!

10. O Indra, thou art more to me than sire or niggard brother is.
Thou and my mother, O good Lord, appear alike, to give me wealth abundantly.

BOOK IV.

CHAPTER I.

DECADE I Indra and others

1. These Soma juice mixt with curd have been expressed for Indra here:
Come with thy bay steeds, Thunder-wielder, to our home, to drink them till they make thee glad!

2. Indra, these Somas with their lauds have been prepared for thy delight.
Drink of the pleasant juice and listen to our songs; lover of song, reward the hymn!

3. I call on thee, Sabardugha, this day, inspirer of the psalm.
Indra, the richly-yielding milch-cow who provides unfailing food in ample stream.

4. Indra, the strong and lofty hills are powerless to bar thy way
None stays that act of thine when thou wouldst fain give wealth to one like me who sings thy praise.

5. Who knows what vital power he wins, drinking beside the flowing juice?
This is the fair-cheeked. God who, joying in the draught, breaks down the castles in his strength.

6. What time thou castest from his seat and punishest the riteless man,
Strengthen for opulence, O Indra Maghavan, our plant desired by many a one!

7. Let Tvashtar, Brahmanaspati, Parjanya guard our heavenly word,
Aditi with her sons, the brothers, guard for us the invincible, the saving word!

8. Ne'er art thou fruitless, Indra, ne'er dost thou desert the worshipper:
But now, O Maghavan, thy bounty as a God is poured forth ever more and
more.

9. Best slayer of the Vritras, yoke thy bay steeds, Indra, far away
Come with the high ones hither, Maghavan, to us, mighty, to, drink the
Soma juice!

10. O Thunderer, zealous worshippers gave thee drink this time yesterday:
So, Indra, listen here to him who offers lauds: come near unto, our
dwelling-place!

DECADE II

1. Advancing, sending forth her rays, the daughter of the Sky is seen.
The mighty one lays bare the darkness with her eye, the friendly Lady
makes the light.

2. These morning sacrifices call you, Asvins, at the break of day.
For help have I invoked you rich in power and might: for, house by house,
ye visit all.

3. Where are ye, Gods? What mortal man, O Asvins, glows with zeal for
you,
Urging you with the crushing stone and with the stalk of Soma thus or
otherwise?

4. This sweetest Soma juice hath been expressed for you at morning rites.
Asvins, drink this prepared ere yesterday and give treasures to him who
offers it!

5. Let me not, still beseeching thee with might and sound of Soma drops,
Anger at sacrifice a fierce wild creature! Who would not beseech the
almighty one!

6. Adhvaryu, let the Soma flow, for Indra longs to drink thereof.
He even now hath yoked his vigorous bay steeds: the Vritraslayer hath come nigh.

7. Bring thou all this unto the good, O Indra, to the old and young!
For, Maghavan, thou art rich in treasures from of old, to be invoked in every fight.

8. If I, O Indra, were the lord of riches ample as thine own,
I would support the singer, God who scatterest wealth! and not abandon him to woe.

9. Thou in thy battles, Indra, art subduer of all hostile bands.
Father art thou, all-conquering, cancelling the curse, thou victor of the vanquisher!

10. For in thy might thou stretchest out beyond the mansions of the sky.
The earthly region, Indra, comprehends thee not. Thou hast waxed mighty over all.

DECADE III

1. Pressed is the juice divine with milk commingled: thereto hath Indra ever been accustomed.
We wake thee, Lord of bays, with sacrifices: mark this our laud in the wild joys of Soma!

2. A home is made for thee to dwell in, Indra: O much-invoked one, with the men go thither!
Thou, that thou mayest guard us and increase us, givest us wealth and joyest in the Somas.

3. The well thou clavest, settest free the fountains, and gavest rest to floods that were obstructed.

Thou, Indra, laying the great mountain open, slaying the Ddnava, didst loose the torrents.

4. When we have pressed the juice we laud thee, Indra, most valorous! even about to win the booty.
Bring us prosperity, and by thy great wisdom, under thine own protection, may we conquer!

5. Thy right hand have we grasped in ours, O Indra, longing, thou very Lord of wealth, for treasures.
Because we know thee, hero, Lord of cattle: vouchsafe us mighty and resplendent riches!

6. Men call on Indra in the armed encounter that he may make the hymns they sing decisive.
Hero in combat and in love of glory, give us a portion of the stall of cattle!

7. Like birds of beauteous wing the Priyamedhas, Rishis, imploring, have come nigh to Indra.
Dispel the darkness and fill full our vision: deliver us as men whom snares entangle!

8. They gaze on thee with longing in their spirit, as on a strongwinged bird that mounteth sky-ward;
On thee with wings of gold, Varuna's envoy, the Bird that hasteneth to the home of Yama.

9. First in the ancient time was Prayer engendered: Vena disclosed the bright ones from the summit,
Laid bare this world's lowest and highest regions, womb of the existent and the non-existent.

10. They have prepared and fashioned for this hero words never matched, most plentiful, most auspicious,

For him the ancient, great, strong, energetic, the very mighty wielder of the thunder.

DECADE IV Indra

1. The black drop sank in Ansumati's bosom, advancing with ten thousand round about it.
Indra with might longed for it as it panted: the hero-hearted King laid down his weapons.

2. Flying in terror from the snort of Vritra all deities who were thy friends forsook thee.
So, Indra, with the Maruts be thy friendship: in all these battles thou shalt be the victor.

3. The old hath waked the young Moon from his slumber who runs his circling course with many round him.
Behold the God's high wisdom in its greatness: he who died yesterday to-day is living.

4. Then, at thy birth, thou wast the foeman, Indra, of those the seven who ne'er had met a rival.
The hidden pair, heaven and the earth, thou foundest, and to the mighty worlds thou gavest pleasure.

5. A friend we count thee, sharp-edged, thunder-wielder, Steer strong of body, overthrowing many.
Thou, helping, causest pious tribes to conquer: Indra, I laud the, heavenly Vritra-slayer.

6. Bring to the wise, the great, who waxeth mighty your offerings,. and make ready your devotion!
Go forth to many tribes as man's controller!

7. Call we on Maghavan, auspicious Indra, best hero in this fight where spoil is gathered,
Strong, listening to give us aid in battles, who slays the Vritras, wins and gathers riches!

8. Prayers have been offered up-through love of glory: Vasishtha, honour Indra in the battle!
He who with fame extends through all existence hears words which I, his faithful servant, utter.

9. May the sweet Soma juices make him happy to cast his quoit that lies in depth of waters!
Thou from the udder which o'er earth Is fastened hast poured the milk into the kine and herbage.

DECADE V Indra and others

1. This vigorous one whom deities commission, the conqueror of cars, the strong and mighty,
Swift, fleet to battle, with uninjured fellics, even Tarkshya for our weal will we call hither.

2. Indra the rescuer, Indra the helper, hero who listens at each Invocation,
Sakra I call, Indra invoked of many. May Indra Maghavan accept our presents!

3. Indra whose right hand wields the bolt we worship, driver of bay steeds seeking sundered courses.
Shaking his beard with might he hath arisen, terrible with his weapons, with his bounty.

4. The ever-slaying, bold and furious Indra, the bright bolt's Lord, the strong, the great, the boundless,
Who slayeth Vritra and acquireth booty, giver of blessings, Maghavan the bounteous.

5. The man who lies in wait and fights against us, deeming himself a giant or a hero,--
By battle or with strength destroy him, Indra! With thy help, manly-souled! may we be victors!

6. He whom men call when striving with their foemen, or speeding onward in array of battle,
Whom bards incite where heroes win the booty, or in the way to waters, He is Indra.

7. On a high car, O Parvata and Indra, bring pleasant viands, with brave heroes, hither!
Enjoy our presents, Gods, at sacrifices: wax strong by hymns, rejoice in our oblation!

8. In ceaseless flow hath he poured forth his praises, as waters from the ocean's depth, to Indra,
Who to his car on both its sides securely hath fixed the earth and heaven as with an axle.

9. May our friends turn thee hitherward to friendship! Mayst thou approach us even o'er many rivers!
May the Disposer, radiant in this mansion with special lustre, bring the father's offspring!

10. Who yokes to-day unto the pole of Order the strong and passionate steers of checkless spirit,
Health-bringing, bearing in their mouths no fodder? Long shall he live who richly pays their service.

CHAPTER II.

DECADE I Indra

1. The singers hymn thee, they who chant the psalm of praise are lauding thee.
The Brahmans have exalted thee, O Satakratu, like a pole.

2. All sacred-songs have magnified Indra expansive as the sea,
Best of all warriors borne on cars, the Lord of heroes, Lord of strength.

3. This poured libation, Indra, drink, immortal, gladdening, excellent:
Streams of the bright have flowed to thee here at the seat of holy Law.

4. Stone-darting Indra, wondrous God, what wealth thou hast not given me here,
That bounty, treasure-finder! bring, filling full both thy hands, to us!

5. O Indra, hear Tiraschi's call, the call of him who serveth thee!
Satisfy him with wealth of kine and valiant offspring! Great art thou.

6. This Soma hath been pressed for thee, O Indra: bold one, mightiest, come!
May Indra-vigour fill thee full, as Surya fills mid-air with rays

7. Come hither, Indra, with thy bays, come thou to Kanva's eulogy!
Ye by command of yonder Dyaus, God bright by day! have gone to heaven.

8. Song-lover! like a charioteer come songs to thee when Soma flows.
Together, they have called to thee as mother-kine unto their calves.

9. Come now and let us glorify pure Indra with pure Sama hymn!

Let milk-blent juice delight him made stronger with pure, pure songs of praise!

10. That which, most wealthy, makes you rich, in splendours most illustrious,
Soma is pressed: thy gladdening drink, Indra libation's Lord! is this.

DECADE II Indra. Dadhikravan

1. Bring forth oblations to the God who knoweth all who fain would drink,
The wanderer, lagging not behind the hero, coming nigh with speed!

2. To us the mighty, lying in all vital power, who resteth in the deep, who standeth in the east.
Drive thou the awful word away.

3. Even as a car to give us aid, we draw thee nigh to favour us,
Strong in thy deeds, quelling attack, Indra, Lord, mightiest! of the brave.

4. With powers of mighty ones hath he, the friend, the ancient, been equipped,
Through whom our father Manu made prayers efficacious with the Gods.

5. What time the swift and shining steeds, yoked to the chariots, draw them on,
Drinking the sweet delightful juice, there men perform their glorious acts.

6. Him for your sake I glorify as Lord of Strength who wrongeth none,
Indra the hero, mightiest, all-conquering and omniscient.

7. I with my praise have glorified strong Dadhikravan, conquering steed
Sweet may he make our mouths: may he prolong the days we have to live!

8. Render of forts, the young, the wise, of strength unmeasured, was he born,

Sustainer of each sacred rite, Indra, the Thunderer, much-extolled.

DECADE III Indra and others

1. Offer the triple sacred draught to Indu hero-worshipper!
With hymn and plenty he invites you to complete the sacrifice.

2. Those whom they call the attendant pair of Kasyapa who knows the light,
Lords of each holy duty when the wise have honoured sacrifice.

3. Sing, sing ye forth your songs of praise, men, Priya-medhas, sing your songs:
Yea, let young children sing their lauds: yea, glorify our firm stronghold!

4. To Indra must a laud be said, a joy to him who freely gives,
That Sakra may be joyful in our friendship and the juice we pour.

5. Your Lord of might that ne'er hath bent, that ruleth over all mankind,
I call, that he, as he is wont, may aid the chariots and the men.

6. Even he who is thine own, through thought of Heaven, of mortal man who toils,
He with the help of lofty Dyaus comes safe through straits of enmity.

7. Wide, Indra Satakratu, spreads the bounty of thine ample grace:
So, good and liberal giver, known to all men, send us splendid wealth!

8. Bright Ushas, when thy times return, all quadrupeds and bipeds stir,
And round about flock winged birds from all the boundaries of heaven.

9. Ye Gods who yonder have your home amid the luminous realm of heaven,
What count ye right? what endless life? What is the ancient call on you?

10. We offer laud and psalm wherewith men celebrate their holy rites.
They govern at the sacred place and bear the sacrifice to Gods.

DECADE IV Indra

1. Heroes of one accord brought forth and formed for kingship Indra who wins the victory in all encounters,
For power, in firmness, in the field, the great destroyer, fierce and exceeding strong,rstalwart and full of vigour.

2. I trust in thy first wrathful deed, O Indra, when thou slewest Vritra and didst work to profit man;
When the two world-halves fled for refuge unto thee, and earth even trembled at thy strength, O Thunder-armed!

3. Come all with might together to the Lord of heaven, the only one who is indeed the guestof men.
He is the first: to him who fain would come to us all pathways turn; he is in truth the only one.

4. Thine, Indra, praised of many, excellently rich, are we who trusting in thy help draw near to thee.
For none but thou, song-lover, shall receive our lauds: as Earth loves all her creatures, welcome this our hymn!

5. High hymns have sounded forth the praise of Maghavan, supporter of mankind, of Indra meet for lauds;
Him who hath waxen mighty, much-invoked with prayers, immortal one whose praise each day is sung aloud.

6. In perfect unison have all your longing hymns that find the light of heaven sounded forth Indra's praise.
As wives embrace their lord, the comely bridegroom, so they compass Maghavan about that he may help.

7. Make glad with songs that Ram whom many men invoke, worthy hymns of praise, Indra the sea of wealth;
Whose boons spread like the heavens, the - lover of mankind: sing praise to him the Sage, most liberal for our good!

8. I glorify that Ram who finds the light of heaven, whose hundred strong and mighty ones go forth with him.
With prayers may I turn hither Indra to mine aid;-the car which like a swift steed hasteth to the call!

9. Filled full of fatness, compassing all things that be, wide, spacious, dropping meath, beautiful in their form,
The heaven and the earth by Varuna's decree, unwasting, rich in germs, stand parted each from each.

10. As like the Morning, thou hast filled, O Indra, both the earth. and heaven,
So as the mighty one, great King of all the mighty race of men, the Goddess mother brought thee forth, the blessed mother gave thee life.

11. Sing, with oblation, praise to him who maketh glad, who with. Rijisvan drove the dusky brood away!
Let us, desiring help, call him for friendship, him the strong, the Marut-girt, whose right hand wields the bolt!

DECADE V Indra

1. I. When Somas flow thou makest pure, Indra, thy mind that merits laud
For gain of strength that ever grows: for great is he.

2. Sing forth to him whom many men invoke, to him whom many laud:
Invite the potent Indra with your songs of praise

3. We sing this strong and wild delight of thine which conquer; in the fray,
Which, Caster of the Stone! gives room and shines like gold,

4. Whether thou drink the Soma by Vishnu's or Trita Aptya's side,
Or with the Maruts, Indra! quaff the following drops.

5. Come, priest, and of the savoury juice pour forth a yet more gladdening draught:
So is the hero praised who ever prospers us.

6. Pour out the drops for Indra; let him drink the meath of Soma juice!
He through his majesty sends forth his bounteous gifts.

7. Come, sing we praise to Indra, friends! the hero who deserves the laud,
Him who with none to aid o'ercomes all tribes of men.

8. Sing ye a psalm to Indra, sing a great song to the lofty Sage,
To him who maketh prayer, inspired who loveth laud!

9. He who alone bestoweth wealth on mortal man who offereth gifts
Is Indra only, potent Lord whom none resist.

10. Companions, let us learn a prayer to Indra, to the Thunderer,
To glorify your bold and most heroic friend!

BOOK V.

CHAPTER I.

DECADE I Indra Adityas

1. Indra, this might of thine I praise most highly for the sacrifice
That thou, O Lord of Power, dost slay Vritra with might

2. For thee this Soma hath been pressed, in whose wild joy thou madest once
Sambara Divodasa's prey: O Indra, drink!

3. Come unto us, O Indra, dear, still conquering, unconcealable!
Wide as a mountain spread on all sides, Lord of heaven!

4. Joy, mightiest Indra, that perceives, sprung from deep Soma draughts, whereby
Thou smitest down the greedy fiend,-that joy we crave!

5. Adityas, very mighty ones, grant to our children and our seed
This lengthened term of life that they may live long days!

6. Though knowest, Indra, Thunder-armed! how to avoid destructive powers,
As one secure from pitfalls each returning day.

7. Drive ye disease and strife away, drive ye away malignity:
Adityas, keep us far removed from sore distress!

8. Drive Soma, Indra, Lord of bays! and let it cheer thee: the stone, like a well-guided courser,

DECADE II Indra.

1. Still, Indra, from all ancient time rivalless ever and companionless art thou:
Thou seekest friendship but in war.

2. Him who of old hath broucht to us this and that blessing, him I magnify for you,
Even Indra, O my friends, for help.

3. Fail not when marching onward: come hither, like-spirited, stay not far away
Ye who can tame even what is firm!

4. Come hither to the dropping juice, O Lord of cornland. Lord of horses, Lord of kine:
Drink thou the Soma, Soma's Lord!

5. Hero, may we, with thee for friend, withstand the man who pants against us in his wrath,
In fight with people rich In kine!

6. Yea, kin by common ancestry, the Maruts, even the oxen, close united friends!
Are licking one another's back.

7. O Indra, bring great strength to us, bring valour, Satakratu, thou most active, bring
A hero conquering in war!

8. So, Indra, friend of song, do we draw nigh to thee with longing; we have streamed to thee
Coming like floods that follow floods

9. Sitting like birds beside thy meath, mingled with milk, which gladdeneth and exalteth thee,

Indra, to thee we sing aloud.

10. We call on thee, O matchless one! We, seeking help, possessing nothing firm ourselves,
Call on thee, wondrous, Thunder-armed.

DECADE III Indra

1. The juice of Soma thus diffused, sweet to the taste the bright cows drink,
Who travelling in splendour close to mighty Indra's side rejoice, good in their own supremacy.

2. Thus hath the Soma, gladdening draught, produced the prayer that giveth joy:
Thou, mightiest, Thunder-armed, hast driven by force the Dragon from the earth, lauding thine own supremacy.

3. By men hath Indra been advanced, the Vritra-slayer, to joy and strength.
Him only we invoke for help in battles whether great or small: be he our aid in deeds of might!

4. Unconquered strength is only thine, Indra, Stonecaster, Thunder-armed!
When thou with thy surpassing power smotest to death that guileful beast, lauding thine own supremacy.

5. Go forward, meet the foe, be bold; thy bolt of thunder is not checked!
Manliness, Indra, is thy strength. Slay Vritra, make the waters thine, lauding thine own supremacy!

6. When war and battles are on foot, booty is offered to the bold.
Yoke thou thy wildly-rushing bays. Whom wilt thou slay, and whom enrich? Do thou, O Indra, make us rich!

7. Wcll have they eaten and rejoiced; the friends have risen and passed away:

The sages luminous in themselves have praised thee with their latest hymn.
Now, Indra, yoke thy two bay steeds!

8. Graciously listen to our songs. Maghavan, be not negligent!
When wilt thou make us glorious? Make this, only this thine end and aim.
Now, Indra! yoke thy two bay steeds.

9. Within the waters runs the Moon, he with the beauteous wings in heaven.
Ye lightnings with your golden wheels, men find not your abiding-place.
Mark this my woe, ye Earth and Sky!

10. To meet your treasure-bringing car, the mighty car must dear to us.
Asvins, the Rishi is prepared, your worshipper, with songs of praise. Lovers of sweetness, hear my call!

DECADE IV Agni and others.

1. O Agni, God, we kindle thee, refulgent, wasting not away,
That this more glorious fuel may send forth for thee its shine to heaven.
Bring food to those who sing thy praise!

2. With offerings of our own we choose thee, Agni, as our Hotar priest,
Piercing and brightly shining-at your glad carouse-served with trimmed grass at sacrifice. Thou waxest great.

3. O heavenly Dawn, awaken us to ample opulence to-day,
Even as thou didst waken us with Satyasravas, Vayya's son, high born! delightful with thy steeds!

4. Send us a mind that brings delight, send energy and mental power.
Then-at your glad carouse-let men joy in thy love, sweet juice! as kine in pasturage. Thou waxest great,

5. Great, as his nature is, through power, terrible, he hath waxed in strength,
Lord of bay steeds, strong-jawed, sublime, he in joined hands for glory's sake hath grasped his iron thunderbolt.

6. He, Indra, verily will mount the powerful car that finds the kine,
Who thinks upon the well-filled bowl, the tawny coursers' harnesser. Now, Indra, yoke thy two bay steeds!

7. I think of Agni who is kind, whom, as their home, the milch-kine seek:
Whom fleet-foot coursers seek as home, and strong enduring steeds as home. Bring food to those who sing thy praise!

8. No peril, no severe distress, ye Gods, affects the mortal man
Whom Aryaman and Mitra lead, and Varuna, of one accord, beyond his foes.

DECADE V Soma Pavamana

1. Flow forth, O Soma, flow thou onward, sweet to Indra's Mitra's, Pushan's, Bhaga's taste.

2. Run forth to battle, conquering the Vritras; thou speedest to quell the foes like one exacting debts.

3. Flow onward, Soma, as a mighty sea, as Father of the Gods, to every form.

4. Flow onward, Soma, flow for mighty strength, as a strong courser, bathed, to win the prize.

5. Fair Indu hath flowed on for rapturous joy, sage, for good fortune, in the waters' lap.

6. In thee, effused. O Soma, we rejoice ourselves for great supremacy in fight:
Thou, Pavamana, enterest into mighty deeds.

7. Who are these radiant men in serried rank, Rudra's young heroes, too, with noble steeds?

8. Agni, with hymns may we now accomplish that which thou lovest,
Strength, like a horse, auspicious strength with service.

9. The strong youths have come forth to view, to show their strength, God Savitar's quickening energy:
Ye warrior horsemen, win the heavens.

10. Soma, flow splendid with thy copious stream in due succession through the ample fleece.

CHAPTER II.

DECADE I. Indra

1. Giver from all sides, bring to us from every side, thou whom as strongest we entreat!

2. This Brahman, comer at due time, named Indra, is renowned and praised.

3. The Brahmans with their hymns exalting Indra increased his strength that he might slaughter Ahi.

4. Anavas wrought a chariot for thy courser, and Tvashtar, much-invoked! the bolt that gitters:

5. Rest, wealth to him who longs for wealth! the riteless stirs not his love nor wins his way to riches.

6. The cows are ever pure and all-supporting, the Gods are ever free from stain and blemish.

7. With all thy beauty come! The kine approaching with full udders follow on thy path.

8. May we, inhabiting a meath-rich dwelling, increase our wealth, and think of thee, O Indra!

9. The Maruts with fair hymns chant out their praise-song: this Indra, famed and youthful, shouts accordant.

10. Sing to your Indra, mightiest Vritra-slayer, sing to the Sage the song that he accepteth!

DECADE II Agni Indra

1. Observant Agni hath appeared, oblation-bearer with his car.

2. O Agni, be our nearest friend, yea, our protector and our kind deliverer!

3. Like wondrous Bhaga, Agni deals treasure among the mighty.

4. Far off or present even now, send forth thy shouting first of all!

5. Dawn drives away her sister's gloom, and through her excellence makes her retrace her path.

6. May we, with Indra and the Gods to aid us, bring these existing worlds to full completion!

7. Like streams of water on their way, let bounties, Indra, flow from thee!

8. With this may we obtain strength god-appointed, happy with brave sons through a hundred winters!

9. With strength let Mitra, Varuna swell oblations; do thou prepare for us rich food, O Indra!

10. Indra is King of all the world.

DECADE III Indra and others

1. At the Trikadrukas the great and strong enjoyed the barley-brew. With Vishnu did he drink the pressed-out Soma juice, even as he would.
That hath so heightened him the great, the wide to do his mighty work. So did the God attend the God, true Indu Indra who is true.

2. This God who sees for thousands of mankind, the light, the thought of poets, and the Law,
The brilliant one, hath sent forth hither all the Dawns: spotless, one-minded, zealous in their home they dwell, with thought upon the Steer.

3. Come to us, Indra, from afar, conducting us, as, to the gatherings, a Lord of heroes, as an archer King, the heroes' Lord!
We come with gifts of pleasant food, with flowing juice, invoking thee, as sons invite a sire, that we may win the spoil, thee, bounteousest, for gain of spoil.

4. Loudly I call that Indra Maghavan, the mighty, resistless, evermore possessing many glories.
Holy, most liberal, may he lead us on to riches, through songs, and, thunder-armed make all our pathways pleasant!

5. Heard be our prayer! In thought I honour Agni first: now straightway we elect this heavenly company, Indra and Vayu we elect.
For when our latest thought is raised and on Vivasvan centred well, then do our holy songs go forward on their way, our songs as 'twere unto the Gods.

6. To Vishnu, to the mighty whom the Maruts follow, let your hymns born in song go forth, Evayamarut!
To the strong, very holy band adorned with bracelets, that rushes on in joy and ever roars for vigour!

7. With this his golden splendour purifying him, be with his own allies subdues all enemies, as Sura with his own allies.
Cleansing himself with stream of juice he shines forth yellow-hued and red, when with the praisers he encompasses all, forms, with praisers having seven mouths.

8. I praise this God, parent of heaven and earth, exceeding wise, possessed of real energy, giver of treasure, thinker dear to all,

Whose splendour is sublime, whose light shone brilliant in, creation, who, wise and golden-handed, in his beauty mader the sky.

9. Agni I deem our Hotar-priest, munificent wealth-giver, Son of Strength, who, knoweth all that is, even as the Sage who, knoweth all.
Lord of fair rites, a God with form erected turning to the Gods, he, when the flame hath sprung forth from the holy oil, the offered fatness, longs for it as it glows bright.

10. This, Indra! dancer! was thy hero deed, thy first and ancient work, worthy to be told forth in heaven,
Even thine who furtheredst life with a God's own power, freeing the floods. All that is godless may he conquer with his might, and, Lord of Hundred Powers, find for us strength and food!

DECADE IV Soma Pavamana

1. High is thy juice's birth: though set it heaven, on earth it hath obtained dread sheltering power and great renown.

2. In sweetest and most gladdening stream flow pure, O Soma, on thy way, pressed out for Indra, for his drink!

3. Flow onward mighty with thy stream, inspiriting the Maruts' Lord, winning all riches with thy power!

4. Flow onward with that juice of thine most excellent, that brings delight, slaying the wicked, dear to Gods!

5. Three several words are uttered: kine are lowing, cows who give the milk; the tawny-hued goes bellowing on.

6. For Indra girt by Maruts, flow, thou Indu, very rich in meath, to seat thee in the place of song!

7. Strong, mountain-born, the stalk hath been pressed in the streams for rapturous joy. Hawk-like he settles in his home.

8. Gold-hued! as one who giveth strength flow on for Gods to drink, a draught for Vayu and the Marut host!

9. Soma, the dweller on the hills, effused, hath flowed into the sieve. All-bounteous art thou in carouse.

10. The Sage of heaven whose heart is wise, when laid between both hands, with roars, gives us delightful powers of life.

DECADE V Soma Pavamana

1. The rapture-shedding Somas have flowed forth in our assembly, pressed to glorify our liberal lords.

2. The Somas, skilled in song, the waves, have led the water forward, like buffaloes speeding to the woods.

3. Indu flow on, a mighty juice; glorify us among the folk: drive all our enemies away!

4. For thou art strong by splendour: we, O Pavamana, call on thee, the brilliant looker on the light.

5. Indu, enlightener, dear, the thought of poets, hath flowed clearly, like a charioteer who starts the steed.

6. Through our desire of heroes, kine, and horses, potent Soma drops, brilliant and swift, have been effused.
God, working with mankind, flow on; to Indra go thy gladdening juice: to Vayu mount as Law commands!
From heaven hath Pavamana made, as 'twere, the marvellous thunder, and the lofty light of all mankind.

7. Pressed for the gladdening draught the drops flow forth abundantly with song, flow onward with the stream of meath.

8. Reposing on the river's wave, the Sage hath widely flowed around, bearing the bard whom many love.

BOOK VI.

CHAPTER I.

DECADE I Soma Pavamana

1. The Gods have come to Indu well-descended, beautified with milk, the active crusher of the foe.

2. Active, while being purified, he hath assailed all enemies: they deck the Sage with holy hymns.

3. Pouring all glories hither, he, effused, hath passed within the jar: Indu on Indra is bestowed.

4. From the two press-boards is the juice sent, like a car-horse, to the sieve: the steed steps forward to the goal.

5. Impetuous, bright, have they come forth, unwearied in their speed, like bulls, driving the black skin far away.

6. Soma, thou flowest chasing foes, finder of wisdom and delight: drive thou the godless folk afar!
Flow onward with that stream wherewith thou gavest splendour to the Sun, speeding the waters kind to man!

8. Flow onward thou who strengthenedst Indra to slaughter Vritra who compassed and stayed the mighty floods!

9. Flow onward, Indu, with this food for him who in thy wild delights battered the nine-and-ninety down!

10. Flow, pressed, into the filter, speed the heavenly one who winneth wealth, who bringeth booty through our juice!

DECADE II Soma Pavamana

1. The tawny Bull hath bellowed, fair as mighty Mitra to behold: he gleams and flashes with the Sun.

2. We choose to-day that chariot-steed of thine, the strong, that brings us bliss, the guardian, the desire of all.

3. Adhvaryu, to the filter lead the Soma juice expressed with stones: make thou it pure for Indra's drink.

4. Swift runs this giver of delight, even the stream of flowingjuice: Swift runs this giver of delight.

5. Pour hitherward, O Soma, wealth in thousands and heroic strength, and keep renown secure for us!

6. The ancient living ones have come unto a newer resting-place. They made the Sun that he might shine.

7. Soma, flow on exceeding bright with loud roar to the reservoirs, resting in wooden vats, thy home!

8. O Soma, thou, art strong and bright, potent, O God, with potent sway: thou, mighty one, ordainest laws.

9. For food, flow onward with thy stream, cleansed and made bright by sapient men: Indu. with sheen approach the milk!

10. Soma, flow on with pleasant stream, strong and devoted to the Gods, our friend, unto the woollen sieve.

11. By this solemnity, Soma, thou, though great, hast been increased: in joy thou, verily actest like a bull!

12. Most active and benevolent, this Pavamana sent to us for lofty friendship meditates.

13. Indu, to us for this great rite, bearing as 'twere thy wave to Gods, unwearied, thou art flowing on.

14. Chasing our foemen, driving off the godless, Soma floweth on, going to Indra's settled place.

DECADE III Soma Pavamana

1. Cleansing thee, Soma, in thy stream, thou flowest in a watery robe: giver of wealth, thou sittest in the place of Law, O God, a fountain made of gold.

2. Hence sprinkle forth the juice effused, Soma, the best of sacred gifts, who, friend of man, hath run amid the water-streams! He hath pressed Soma out with stones.

3. Expressed by stones, O Soma, and urged through the long wool of the sheep, thou, entering the press-boards even as men a fort, gold-hued hast settled in the vats.

4. O Soma,--for the feast of Gods, river-like he hath swelled with surge, sweet with the liquor of the stalk, as one who wakes, into the vat that drops with meath.

5. Pressed out by pressers, Soma goes over the fleecy backs of sheep, goes, even as with a mare, in tawny-coloured stream, goes in a sweetly-sounding stream.

6. O Soma, Indu, every day thy friendship hath been my delight. Many fiends follow me help me, thou tawny-hued: pass on beyond these barriers!

7. Deft-handed! thou when purified liftest thy voice amid the sea. Thou, Pavamana, makest riches flow to us, yellow, abundant, much desired.

8. The living drops of Soma juice pour, as they flow, the gladdening drink, intelligent drops above the station of the sea, exhilarating, dropping meath.

9. Soma, while thou art cleansed, most dear and watchful in the sheep's long wool, most like to Angiras! thou hast become a sage. Sprinkle our sacrifice with mead!

10. Soma, the gladdening juice, flows pressed for Indra with his Marut host: he hastens o'er the fleece with all his thousand streams: him, him the men make pure and bright.

11. Flow on, best winner of the spoil, to precious gifts of every sort! Thou art a sea according to the highest law, joy-giver, Soma! to the Gods

12. Over the cleansing sieve have flowed the Pavamanas in a stream, girt by the Maruts, gladdening, steeds with Indra's strength, for wisdom and for dainty food.

DECADE IV Soma Pavamana

1. Run onward to the reservoir and seat thee: cleansed by the men speed forward to the battle!
Making thee glossy like an able courser, forth to the sacred grass with reins they lead thee.

2. The God declares the deities' generations, like Uaana, proclaiming lofty wisdom.
With brilliant kin, far-ruling, sanctifying, the wild boar, singing with his foot, advances.

3. Three are the voices that the car-steed utters: he speaks the lore of prayer, the thought of Order.

To the cows' master come the cows inquiring: the hymns with eager longing come to Soma.

4. Made pure by this man's urgent zeal and impulse, the God hath with his juice the Gods pervaded.
Pressed, singing, to the sieve he goes, as passes the Hotar to enclosures holding cattle.

5. Father of holy hymns Soma flows onward, the father of the earth, father of heaven;
Father of Agni, Surya's generator, the father who begat Indra and Vishnu

6. To him, praiseworthy, sacred tones have sounded, Steer of the triple height, the life-bestower.
Dwelling in wood, like Varuna, a river, lavishing treasure, he distributes blessings.

7. Guard of all being, generating creatures, loud roared the sea as highest law commanded.
Strong, in the filter, on the fleecy summit, pressed from the stone, Soma hath waxen mighty.

8. Loud neighs the tawny steed when started, settling deep in the wooden vessel while they cleanse him.
Led by the men he makes the milk his raiment; then shall he, of himself, engender worship.

9. This thine own Soma, rich in meath, O Indra, the Strong, hath flowed into the Strong One's filter.
The swift steed, bounteous, giving hundreds, thousands, hath reached the sacred grass which never fails him.

10. Flow onward, Soma, rich in meath, and holy, enrobed in waters, on the fleecy summit!

Settle in vessels that are full of fatness, as cheering and most gladdening drink for Indra!

DECADE V Soma Pavamana

1. In forefront of the cars forth goes the hero, the leader, seeking spoil: his host rejoices.
Soma endues his robe of lasting colours, and blesses, for his friends, their calls on Indra.

2. Thy streams have been poured forth with all their sweetness, when, cleansed thou passest through the woollen filter.
The race of kine thou cleansest, Pavamana! Thou didst beget: and speed the Sun with splendours.

3. Let us sing praises to the Gods: sing loudly, send ye the Soma forth for mighty riches!
Let him flow, sweetly-flavoured, through the filter: let the God Indu settle in the beaker!

4. Urged on, the father of the earth and heaven hath gone forth like a car to gather booty.
Going to Indra, sharpening his weapons, and in his hands containing every treasure.

5. When, by the law of the Most High, in presence of heaven and earth, the fond mind's utterance formed him.
Then, loudly lowing, came the cows to Indu, the chosen, wellloved master in the beaker.

6. Ten sisters, pouring out the rain together, the sage's quickly-moving thoughts, adorn him.
Hither hath run the gold-hued child of Surya, and reached the vat like a fleet vigorous courser.

7. When beauties strive for him as for a charger, then strive the songs as people for the sunlight.
A mighty Sage, he flows enrobed in waters and hymns as 'twree a stall that kine may prosper.

8. Strong Indu, bathed in milk, flows on for Indra, Soma exciting, strength, for his carousal.
He quells malignity and slays the demons, King of the homestead, he who gives us comfort.

9. Pour forth this wealth with this purification: flow onward to the yellow lake, O Indu!
Here, too, the bright one, wind-swift, full of wisdom, shall give a son to him who cometh quickly.

10. Soma, the mighty, when, the waters' offspring, he chose the Gods, performed that great achievement.
He, Pavamana, granted strength to Indra: he, Indu, generated light in Surya.

11. As for a chariot-race, the skilful speaker, first hymn, inventor, hath with song been started.
The sisters ten upon the fleecy summit adorn the car-horse in the resting-places.

12. Hastening onward like the waves of waters our holy hymns are coming forth to Soma.
To him they go with lowly adoration, and, longing, enter him who longs to meet them.

CHAPTER II.

DECADE I Soma Pavamana

1. For first possession of your juice. for the exhilarating drink,
Drive ye away the dog, my friends, drive ye the long-tongued dog away!

2. As Pushan. Fortune, Bhaga, comes this Soma while they make him pure.
He, Lord of all the multitude, hath looked upon the earth and heaven.

3. The Somas, very rich in sweets, for which the sieve is destined,. flow
Effused, the source of Indra's joy: may your strong juices reach the Gods!

4. For us the Soma juices flow, the drops best furtherers of weal,
Effused as friends, without a spot, benevolent, finders of the. light.

5. Stream on us riches that are craved by hundreds, best at winning spoil,
Riches, O Indu, thousandfold, most splendid, that surpass the light!

6. The guileless ones are singing praise to Indra's well-beloved friend,
As, in the morning of its life, the mothers lick the new-born calf.

7. They for the bold and lovely one ply manly vigour like a bow;
Bright, glad, in front of songs they spread to form a vesture for the Lord.

8. Him with ths fleece they purify, brown, golden-hued, beloved of all,
Who with exhilarating juice goes forth to all the deities.

9. Let him, as mortal, crave this speech, for him who presses, of the juice,
As Bhrigu's sons chased Makha, so drive ye the niggard hound away!

DECADE II Soma Pavamana

1. Graciously-minded he is flowing on his way to win dear names o'er which the youthful one grows great.
The mighty and far-seeing one hath mounted now the mighty Surya's car which moves to every side.

2. Spontaneous let our drops of Soma juice flow on, pressed out and tawny-coloured, mightily, to the Gods!
Still let our enemies, the godless, be in want, though filled with food; and let our prayers obtain success!

3. Most beauteous of the beauteous, Indra's thunderbolt, this Soma, rich in sweets, hath clamoured in the vat.
Dropping with oil, abundant, streams of sacrifice flow unto him, and milch-kine, lowing, with their milk.

4. Indu hath started forth for Indra's settled place, and slights not, as a friend, the promise of his friend.
Soma comes onward like a youth with youthful maids, and gains the beaker by a course of hundred paths.

5. On flows the potent juice, sustainer of the heavens; the strength of Gods, whom men must hail with shouts of joy.
Thou, gold-hued, started like a courser by brave men, art lightly showing forth thy splendour in the streams.

6. Far-seeing Soma flows, the Steer, the Lord of hymns, the furtherer of days, of mornings, and of heaven.
Breath of the rivers, he hath roared into the jars, and with the help of sages entered Indra's heart.

7. The three-times seven milch-kine in the loftiest heaven have for this Soma poured the genuine milky draught.
Four other beauteous creatures hath he made for his adornment when he waxed in strength through holy rites.

8. Flow on to indra, Soma, carefully effused: let sickness stay afar together with the fiend!
Let not the double-tongued delight them with thy juice: here be thy flowing drops laden with opulence!

9. Even as a King hath Soma, red and tawny Bull, been pressed: the wondrous one hath bellowed to the kine.
While purified thou passest through the filtering fleece to seat thee hawk-like on the place that drops with oil.

10. The drops of Soma juice, like cows who yield their milk, have flowed forth, rich in meath, unto the diety,
And, seated on the grass, raising their voice, assumed the milk, the covering robe wherewith the address stream.

11. They balm him, balm him over, balm him thoroughly, caress the mighty strength and balm it with the meath.
They seize the flying Steer at the stream's breathing-place: cleansing with gold they grasp the animal herein.

12. Spread is thy cleansing filter, Brahmanaspati: as prince thou enterest its limbs from every side.
The raw, whose mass hath not been heated, gains not this: they only which are dressed, which bear, attain to it.

DECADE III Soma Pavamana

1. To Indra, to the mighty one, let these gold-coloured juices go,
Drops born as Law prescribes, that find the light of heavenj

2. Flow vigilant for Indra, thou Soma, yea, Indu, run thou forth;
Bring hither splendid strength that finds the light of heaven!

3. Sit down, O friends, and sing aloud to him who purifies himself.

Deck him for glory, like a child, with holy rites!

4. Friends, hymn your Lord who makes him pure for rapturous
carouse: let them
Sweeten him, as a child, with lauds and sacred gifts!

5. Breath of the mighty Dames, the Child, speeding the plan of' sacrifice,
Surpasses all things that are dear, yea, from of old!

6. In might, O Indu, with thy streams flow for the banquet of the Gods:
Rich in meath, Soma, in our beaker take thy seat!

7. Soma, while filtered, with his wave flows through the long wool of the
sheep,
Roaring, while purified, before the voice of song.

8. The speech is uttered for the Sage, for Soma being purified:
Bring meed as 'twere to one who makes thee glad with hymns!

9. Flow to us, Indu, very strong, effused, with wealth of kine and, steeds,
And do thou lay above the milk thy radiant hue!

10. Voices have sung aloud to thee as finder-out of wealth for us:
We clothe the hue thou wearest with a robe of milk.

11. Gold-hued and lovely in his course through tangles of the wooli he
flows:
Stream forth heroic fame upon the worshippers!

12. On through the long wool of the sheep to the meath-dropping vat he
flows:
The Rishis' sevenfold quire hath sung aloud to him.

DECADE IV Soma Pavamana

I. For Indra flow, thou Soma, on, as most inspiring drink, exceeding rich in sweets.
Great, most celestial, gladdening drink!

2. Make high and splendid glory shine hitherward, Lord of food, God, on the friend of Gods:
Unclose the cask of middle air!

3. Press ye and pour him, like a steed, laud-worthy, speeding through the region and the flood,
Who swims in water, dwells in wood!

4. Him, even this Steer who milks the heavens, him with a thousand streams, distilling rapturous joy,
Him who brings all things excellent.

5. Effused is he who brings good things, who brings us store of' wealth and sweet refreshing food,
Soma who brings us quiet homes.

6. For, verily, Pavamana, thou, divine! endued with brightest splendour calling all
Creatures to immortality.

7. Effused, he floweth in a stream, best rapture-giver, in the longwool of the sheep,
Sporting, as 'twere the waters' wave.

8. He who from out the rocky cavern with his might took forth the red-refulgent cows--
Thou drewest to thyself the stall of kine and steeds: burst it,
brave Lord, like one in mail; yea, burst it, O brave Lord, like one in mail!

PART SECOND

BOOK I.

CHAPTER I.

Om. Glory to the Samaveda! to Lord Ganesa glory! Om.

I Soma Pavamana

1. Sing forth to Indu, O ye men, to him who now is purified,
Fain to pay worship to the Gods!

2, Together with thy pleasant juice the Atharvans have commingled. milk.
Divine, God-loving, for the God.

3. Bring health to cattle with thy flow, health to the people, health, to
steeds,
Health, O thou King, to growing plants!

II Soma Pavamana

1. Bright are these Somas blent with milk, with light that flashes brilliantly,
And form that shouteth all around.

2. Roused by his drivers and sent forth, the strong Steed hath come: nigh
for spoil,
As warriors when they stand arrayed.

3. Specially, Soma, Sage, by day, coming together for our weal,
Like Surya, flow for us to see!

III Soma Pavamana

1. The streams of Pavamana, thine, Sage, mighty one, have poured them
forth,

Like coursers eager for renown.

2. They have been poured upon the Reece towards the meath-distilling vat:
The holy songs have rung aloud.

3. Like milch-kine coming home, the drops of Soma juice have reached the lake,
Have reached the shrine of sacrifice

IV Agni

1. Come, Agni, praised with song to feast and sacrificial offerings: sit
As Hotar on the holy grass!

2. So, Angiras, we make thee strong with fuel and with holy oil.
Blaze high, thou youngest of the Gods!

3. For us thou winnest, Agni, God, heroic strength exceeding great, Far-
spreading and of high renown.

V Mitra Varuna

1. Varuna, Mitra, sapient pair, pour fatness on our pastures, pour
Meath on the regions of the air!

2, Gladdened by homage, ruling far, ye reign by majesty of might,
Pure in your ways, for evermore.

3. Lauded by Jamadagni's song, sit in the shrine of sacrifice:
Drink Soma, ye who strengthen Law!

VI Indra

1. Come, we have pressed theJuice for thee; O Indra, drink this Soma here:
Sit thou on this my sacred grass!

2. O Indra, let thy long-maned bays, yoked by prayer, bring thee hitherward!
Give ear and listen to our prayers!

3. We Soma-bearing Brahmans call thee Soma-drinker with thy friend,
We, Indra, bringing Soma juice.

VII Indra Agni

1. Indra and Agni, moved by songs, come to the juice, the precious dew:
Drink ye thereof, impelled by prayer!

2. Indra and Agni, with the man who lauds comes visible sacrifice:
So drink ye both this flowing juice!

3. With force of sacrifice I seek Indra, Agni who love the wise:
With Soma let them sate them here!

VIII Soma Pavamana

1. High is thy juice's birth: though set in heaven, on earth it hath obtained
Dread sheltering power and great renown.

2. Finder of room and freedom, flow for Indra whom we must adore,
For Varuna and the Marut host!

3. Striving to win, with him we gain all riches from the enemy,
Yea, all the glories of mankind,

IX Soma Pavamana

1. Cleansing thee, Soma, in thy stream, thou flowest in watery robe.
Giver of wealth, thou sittest in the place of Law, O God, a fountain made of
gold.

2. He, milking for dear meath the heavenly udder, hath sat in the ancient gathering-place.

Washed by the men, far-sighted, strong, thou streamest to ther honourable reservoir.

X Soma Pavamana

1. Run onward to the reservoir and seat thee: cleansed by the men speed forward to the battle.

Making thee glossy like an able courser, forth to the sacred grass with reins they lead thee.

2. Indu, the well-armed God is flowing onward, he who averts the curse and guards the homesteads.

Father, begetter of the Gods, most skilful, the buttress of the heavens and earth's supporter.

XI Indra

1. Like kine unmilked we call aloud, hero, to thee, and sing thy
praise,

Looker on heavenly light, Lord of this moving world, Lord, Indra! of what moveth not.

2. None other like to thee, of earth or of the heavens, hath been or ever will be born.

Desiring horses, Indra Maghavan! and kine, as men of might we call on thee.

XII Indra

1. With what help will he come to us, wonderful, everwaxing friend?
With what most mighty company?

2. What genuine and most liberal draught will spirit thee with juice to burst
Open e'en strongly-guarded wealth?

3. Do thou who art protector of us thy friends who praise thee
With hundred aids approach us!

XIII Indra

1. As cows low to their calves in stalls, so with our songs we glorify
This Indra, even your wondrous God who checks attack, who takes delight
in precious juice.

2. Celestial, bounteous giver, girt about with might, rich, mountain-like, in
pleasant things,--
Him swift we seek for foodful booty rich in kine, brought hundredfold and
thousandfold.

XIV Indra

1. Loud-singing at tbe sacred rite where Soma flows, we priests invoke.
With haste, that he may help, as the bard's cherisher. Indra who findeth
wealth for you.

2. Whom, fair of cheek, in rapture of the juice, the firm resistless slayers
hinder not:
Giver of glorious wealth to him who sings his praise, honouring him who
toils and pours.

XV Soma Pavamana

1. In sweetest and most gladdening stream flow pure, O Soma, on thy way,
Pressed out for Indra, for his drink!

2. Fiend-queller, friend of all men, he hath reached his shrine, his dwelling-
place.

Within the iron-hammered vat.

3. Be thou best Vritra-slayer, best granter of room, most liberal:
Promote our wealthy princes' gifts!

XVI Soma Pavamana

1. For Indra flow, thou Soma, on, as most inspiring drink, most rich in sweets,
Great, most Celestial, gladdening drink!

2. Thou of whom having drunk the Steer acts like a steer: having drunk this that finds the light,
He, excellently wise, hath come anear to food and booty, even as Etasa.

XVII Indra

1. To Indra, to the mighty let these golden-coloured juices go,
Drops born as Law prescribes, that find the light of heaven!

2. This juice that gathers spoil flows, pressed, for Indra, for his maintenance.
Soma bethinks him of the conqueror, as he knows.

3. Yea, Indra in the joys of this obtains the grasp that gathers spoil,
And, winning waters, wields the mighty thunderbolt.

XVIII Soma Pavamana.

1. For first possession of your juice, for the exhilarating drink,
Drive ye away the dog, my friends, drive ye the long-tongued dog away!

2. He who with purifying stream, effused, comes flowing hitherward,
Indu, is like an able steed.

3. With prayer all-reaching let the men tend unassailable Soma: be-
The stones prepared for sacrifice!

XIX Soma Pavamana

1. Graciously- minded he is flowing on his way to win dear names o'er
which the youthful one grows great.
The mighty and far-seeing one hath mounted now the mighty
Surya's car which moves to every side.

2. The speaker, unassailable master of this prayer, the tongue of sacrifice,
pours forth the pleasant meath.
As son be sets the name of mother and of sire in the far distance, in the
third bright realm of heaven.

3. Sending forth flashes he hath bellowed to the jars, led by the men into
the golden reservoir.
The milkers of the sacrifice have sung to him: Lord of three heights, thou
shinest brightly o'er the Dawns.

XX Agni

1. Sing to your Agni with each song, at every sacrifice for strength!
Come, let us praise the wise and everlasting God, even as a well-beloved
friend:

2. The Son of Strength; for is be not our gracious Lord? Let us serve him
who bears our gifts!
In battles may he be our help and strengthener, yea, be the saviour of our
lives!

XXI Agni

1. O Agni, come; far other songs of praise will I sing forth to thee.
Wax mighty with these Soma drops!

2. Where'er thy mind applies itself, vigour preeminent hast thou:
There wilt thou gain a dwelling-place.

3. Not for a moment only lasts thy bounty, Lord of many men:
Our service therefore shalt thou gain.

XXII Indra

1. We call on thee, O matchless one. We, seeking help, possessing nothing firm ourselves.
Call on thee, wondrous, thunder-armed:

2. On thee for aid in sacrifice, This youth of ours, the bold, the terrible, bath gone forth.
We therefore, we thy friends, Indra, have chosen thee, spoil winner, as our succourer.

XXIII Indra

1. So, Indra, friend of song, do we draw near to thee with longing; we have streamed to thee
Coming like floods that follow floods.

2. As rivers swell the ocean, so, hero, our prayers increase thy might,
Though of thyself, O Thunderer, waxing day by day.

3. With holy song they bind to the broad wide-yoked car the bay steeds of the quickening God,
Bearers of Indra, yoked by word.

CHAPTER II.

I Indra

I. Invite ye Indra with a song to drink your draught of Soma juicel
All-conquering Satakratu, most munificent of all who live!

2. Lauded by many, much-invoked, leader of song renowned of old:
His name is Indra, tell it forth!

3. Indra, the dancer, be to us the giver of abundant wealth:
The mighty bring it us knee-deep!

II Indra

1. Sing ye a song, to make him glad, to Indra, Lord of tawny steeds,
The Soma-drinker, O my friends!

2. To him, the bounteous, say the laud, and let us glorify, as men
May do, the giver of true gifts!

3. O Indra, Lord of boundless might, for us thou seekest spoil and kine,
Thou seekest gold for us, good Lord!

III Indra

1. This, even this, O Indra, we implore: as thy devoted friends,
The Kanvas praise thee with their hymns.

2. Naught else, O Thunderer, have I praised in the skilled singer's eulogy;
On thy laud only have I thought.

3. The Gods seek him who presses out the Soma; they desire not sleep:
They punish sloth unweariedly

IV Indra

1. For Indra, lover of carouse, loud be our songs about the juice:
Let poets sing the song of praise

2. We summon Indra to the draught, in whom all glories rest, in whom
The seven communities rejoice.

3. At the Trikadrukas the Gods span sacrifice that stirs the mind:
Let our songs aid and prosper it!

V Indra

1. Here, Indra, is thy Soma draught, made pure upon the sacred grass:
Run hither, come and drink thereof!

2. Strong-rayed! adored with earnest hymns! this juice is shed for thy delight:
Thou art invoked, Akhandala!

3. To Kundapayya, grandson's son, grandson of Sringavrish! to thee,
To him have I addressed my thought.

VI Indra

1. Indra, as one with mighty arm, gather for us with thy right hand,
Manifold and nutritious spoil!

2. We know thee mighty in thy deeds, of mighty bounty, mighty wealth.
Mighty in measure, prompt to aid.

3. Hero when thou wouldst give thy gifts, neither the Gods nor mortal men

Restrain thee like a fearful bull.

VII Indra

1. Hero, the Soma being shed, I pour the juice for thee to drink:
Sate thee and finish thy carouse!

2. Let not the fools, or those who mock, beguile thee when they seek thine aid:
Love not the enemy of prayer!

3. Here let them cheer thee well supplied with milk to great munificence:
Drink as the wild bull drinks the lake!

VIII Indra

I. Here is the Soma juice expressed: O Vasu, drink till thou art full!
Undaunted God, we give it thee!

2. Washed by the men, pressed out with stones, strained through the filter made of wool,
'Tis like a courser bathed in streams.

3. This juice have we made sweet for thee like barley, blending it with milk.
Indra, I call thee to our feast.

IX Indra

1. So, Lord of affluent gifts, this juice hath been expressed for thee with strength:
Drink of it, thou who lovest song!

2. Incline thy body to the juice which suits thy godlike nature well:
Thee, Soma-lover! let it cheer!

3. O Indra, let it enter both thy flanks, enter thy head with prayer,
With bounty, hero! both thine arms!

X Indra

1. O Come ye hither, sit ye down; to Indra sing ye forth your song,
Companions, bringing hymns of praise,

2. Laud Indra, richest of the rich, who ruleth over noblest wealth,
Beside the flowing Soma juice!

3. May he stand near us in our need with all abundance, for our wealth:
With strength may he come nigh to us!

XI Indra

1. In every need, in every fray we call, as friends to succour us,
Indra, the mightiest of all.

2. I call him, mighty to resist, the hero of our ancient home,
Thee whom my sire invoked of old.

3. If he will hear us, let him come with succour of a thousand kinds,
With strength and riches, to our call!

XI Indra

1. When Somas flow thou makest pure, Indra, thy mind that merits laud,
For gain of strength that ever grows: for great is he.

2. In heaven's first region, in the seat of Gods, is he who brings success,
Most glorious, prompt to save, who wins the waterfloods.

3. Him I invoke, to win the spoil, even mighty Indra for the fray.
Be thou most near to us for bliss, a friend to aid!

XIII Agni

1. With this mine homage I invoke Agni for you, the Son of Strength.
Dear, wisest envoy, skilled in noble sacrifice, immortal, messanger of all.

2. His two red horses, all-supporting, let him yoke: let him, well-worshipped, urge them fast!
Then hath the sacrifice good prayers and happy end, the heavenly gift of wealth to men.

XIV Dawn

1. Advancing, sending forth her rays, the daughter of the Sky is seen.
The mighty one lays bare the darkness with her eye, the friendly Lady makes the light.

2. The Sun ascending, the refulgent star, pours down his beams. together with the Dawn.
O Dawn, at thine arising, and, the Sun's, may we attain the share allotted us!

XV Asvins

1. These morning sacrifices call you, Asvins, at the break of day.
For help have I invoked you rich in power and might: for, house by house, ye visit all.

2. Ye, heroes, have bestowed wonderful nourishment: send it to him whose songs are sweet.
One-minded, both of you, drive your car down to us: drink yethe savoury Soma juice!

XVI Soma Pavamana.

1. After his ancient splendour, they, the bold, have drawn the bright milk from

The Sage who wins a thousand spoils.

2. In aspect he is like the Sun: he runneth forward to the lakes: Seven currents flowing to the sky.

3. He, while they purify him, stands high over all things that exist Soma, a God as Surya is.

XVII Soma Pavamana

1. By generation long ago this God, engendered for the Gods,
Flows tawny to the straining cloth.

2. According to primeval plan this poet hath been strengthened by,
The sage as God for all the Gods.

3. Shedding the ancient fiuid thou art poured into the cleansing sieve:
Roaring, thou hast produced the Gods.

XVIII Soma Pavamana

1. Bring near us those who stand aloof: strike fear into our enemy:
O Pavamana, find us wealth!

2. To him the active, nobly born.

3. Sing ye your songs to him, O men!

XIX Soma Pavamana

1. The Somas skilled in song, the waves have led the water forward, like Buffaloes speeding to the woods.

2. With stream of sacrifice the brown bright drops have flowed with strength in store
Of kine into the wooden vats.

3. To Indra, Vayu. Varuna to Vishnu and the Maruts let
The Soma juices flow expressed.

XX Soma Pavamana

1. O Soma, for the feast of Gods, river-like he hath swelled with surge,
Sweet with the liquor of the stalk, as one who wakes, into the vat that drops with meath.

2. Like a dear son how must be decked, the bright and shining one hath clad him in his robe.
Men skilful at their work drive him forth, like a car, into the rivers from their hands.

XXI Soma Pavamana

1. The rapture-shedding Somas have flowed forth in our assembly, pressed.
To glorify our liberal lords.

2. Now like a swan hemaketh all the company sing each his hymm
He like steed is bathed in milk.

3. And Trita's maidens onward urge the tawny-coloured with the stones,
Indu for Indra, for his drink.

XXII Soma Pavamana.

1. Herewith flow on, thou friend of Gods! Singing, thou runnest round the sieve oni every side.
The streams of meath have been effused.

2. Lovely, gold-coloured, on he flows.

For him who presses, of the juice.

BOOK II.

CHAPTER I.

I Soma Pavamana

1. Soma, as leader of the song, flow onward with thy wondrous aid.
For holy lore of every sort!

2. Do thou as leader of the song, stirring the waters of the sea,
Flow onward, known to all mankind!

1 O Soma, O thou Sage, these worlds stand ready to enhance thy might:
The milch-kine run for thy behoof.

II Soma Pavamana

1. Indu, flow on, a mighty juice; glorify us among the folk:
Drive all our enernies away!

2. And in thy friendship, Indu, most sublime and glorious, may we
Subdue all those who war with us!

3. Those awful weapons which thou hast, sharpened at point to strike men down--
Guard us therewith from every foe!

III Soma Pavamana

1. O Soma, thou art strong and bright, potent, O God, with potent sway,

2. Steer-strong thy might is like a steer's, steer-strong the wood, steer-strong the juice:
A steer indeed, O Steer, art thou.

3. Thou, Indu, as a vigorous horse, hast neighed together steeds and kine:
Unbar for us the doors to wealth!

IV Soma Pavamana

1. For thou art strong by splendour: we, O Pavamana call on thee,
The brilliant looker on the light.

2. When thou art sprinkled with the streams, thou reachest, purified by men,
Thy dwelling in the wooden vat.

3. Do thou, rejoicing, nobly-armed! pour upon us heroic strength.
O Indu, come thou hitherward!

V Soma Pavamana

1. We seek to win thy friendly love, even Pavamana's flowing o'er
The limit of the cleansing sieve.

2. With those same waves which in their stream o'erflow the purifying sieve,
Soma, be gracious unto us!

3. O Soma, being purified, bring us from all sides-for thou canst-
Riches and food with hero sons!

VI Agni

1. Agni we choose as envoy, skilled performer of this holy rite,
Hotar, possessor of all wealth.

2. With constant calls they invocate Agni, Agni, Lord of the house,
Oblation-bearer, much-beloved

3. Bring the Gods hither, Agni, born for him who trims the Sacred grass:
Thou art our Hotar, meet for praise!

VII Mitra Varuna

1. Mitra and Varuna we call to drink the draught of Soma juice,
Those born endowed with holy strength.

2. Those who by Law uphold the Law, Lords of the shining light of Law,
Mitra I call, and Varuna.

3. Let Varuna be our chief defence, let Mitra guard us with all aids,
Both make us rich exceedingly!

VIII Indra

1. Indra the singers with high praise, Indra reciters with their lauds,
Indra the choirs have glorified.

2. Indra is close to his two bays, with chariot ready at his word,
Indra the golden, thunder-armed.

3. Help us in battles Indra, in battles where thousand spoils are gained,
With awful aids, O awful one!

4. Indra raised up the son aloft in heaven, that he may see afar:
He burst the mountain for the kine.

IX Indra-Agni

1. To Indra and to Agni we bring reverence high and holy hymn,
And, craving help, soft words with prayer.

2. For all these holy singers thus implore these twain to succour them,

And priests that they may win them strength.

3. Eager to laud you, we with songs invoke you, bearing sacred food,
Fain for success in sacrifice.

X Soma Pavamana

1. Flow onward, mighty with thy stream, inspiriting the Marut's Lord,
Winning all riches with thy power!

2. I send thee forth to battle from the press, O Pavamana, strong,
Sustainer, looker on the light!

3. Acknowledged by this song of mine, flow, tawnycoloured, with thy stream:
Incite to battle thine ally!

XI Soma Pavamana

1. A Red Bull bellowing to the kine, thou goest, causing the heavens and earth to roar and thunder.
A shout is heard like Indra's in the battle: thou flowest on, sending this voice before thee.

2. Swelling with milk, abounding in sweet juices, urging the meathrich plant thou goest onward.
Making loud clamour, Soma Pavamana, thou flowest when thou art effused for Indra.

3. So flow thou on inspiriting, for rapture, turning the weapon of the water's holder!
Flow to us wearing thy resplendent colour, effused and eager for the kine.
O Soma!

XII Indra

1. That we may win us wealth and power we poets verily, call on thee:
In war men call on thee, Indra, the hero's Lord, in the steed's race-course
call on thee

2. As such, O wonderful, whose hand holds thunder, praised as mighty,
Caster of the Stone!
Pour on us boldly, Indra, kine and chariot-steeds, ever to be the conque-
ror's strength!

XIII Indra

1. To you will I sing Indra's praise who gives good gifts, as we I we know;
The praise of Maghavan who, rich in treasure, aids his singers with wealth
thousandfold.

2. As with a hundred hosts, he rushes boldly on, and for the offerer slays
his foes.
As from a mountain fiow the water-brooks, thus flow his gifts who feedeth
many a one.

XIV Indra

1. O Thunderer, zealous worshippers gave thee drink this time yesterday:
So, Indra, listen here to him who offers lauds: come near unto our dwelling-
place!

2. Lord of bay steeds, fair-helmed, rejoice thee: thee we seek. Here the
disposers wait on thee.
Thy glories, meet for praise! are highest by the juice, O Indra, lover of the
song.

XV Soma Pavamana

1. Flow onward with that juice of thine most excellent, that brings delight,

Slaying the wicked, dear to Gods!

2. Killing the foeman and his hate, and daily winning spoil and strength,
Gainer art thou of steeds and kine.

3. Red-hued, be blended with the milk that seems to yield its lovely breast,
Falcon-like resting in thine home!

XVI Soma Pavamana

1. As Pashan, Fortune, Bhaga, comes this Soma while they make him pure.
He, Lord of all the multitude, hath looked upon the earth and heaven.

2. The dear cows sang in joyful mood together to the gladdening drink.
The drops as they are purified, the Soma juices, make the paths.

3. O Pavamana, bring the Juice, the mightiest, worthy to be famed,
Which the Five Tribes have over them, whereby we may win opulence!

XVII Soma Pavamana

1. Far-seeing Soma flows, the Steer, the Lord of hymns, the furtherer of
days, of mornings, and of heaven.
Breath of the rivers, he hath roared into the jars, and with the help of sages
entered Indra's heart.

2. On, with the sages, flows the poet on his way, and guided by the men,
hath streamed into the vats.
He, showing Trita's name, hath caused the meath to flow, increasing Vayu's
strength to make him Indra's friend.

3. He, being purified, hath made the mornings shine, and it is he who gave
the rivers room to flow.
Making the three-times seven pour out the milky stream, Soma, the
cheerer, yields whate'er the heart finds sweet.

XVIII Indra

1. For so thou art the brave man's friend; a hero, too, art thou, and strong:
So may thy heart be won us!

2. So hath the offering. wealthiest Lord, been paid by all the worshippers.
So dwell thou, Indra, even with us!

3. Be not thou like a slothful priest, O Lord of spoil and strength: rejoice
In the pressed Soma blent with milk!

XIX Indra

1. All sacred songs have magnified Indra expansive as the sea.
Best of all warriors borne on cars, the Lord of heroes, Lord of strength.

2. Lord of might, Indra, may we ne'er, strong in thy friendship, be afraid!
We glorify with praises thee, the never conquered conqueror.

3. The gifts of Indra from of old, his saving succours never fail,
When to his worshippers he gives the boon of booty rich in kine.

CHAPTER II.

I Soma Pavamana

1. These rapid Soma-drops have been poured through the purifying sieve.
To bring us all felicities.

2. Dispelling manifold mishap, giving the courser's progeny,
Yea, and the warrior steed's, success.

3. Bringing prosperity to kine, they pour perpetual strengthening food
On us for noble eulogy.

II Soma Pavamana.

1. King Pavamana is implored with holy songs, on man's behalf,
To travel through, the realm of air.

2. Pressed for the banquet of the Gods, O Soma, bring us might,and speed,
Like beauty for a'brilliant show!

3. Bring us, O Indu, hundredfold increase of kine, and noble steeds.
The gift of fortune for our help!

III Soma Pavamana

1. With sacrifice we seek to thee fair cherisher of manly might
In mansons of the lofty heavens.

2. Drink gladdening, crusher of the bold, praiseworthy, with most mighty
sway,

Destroyer of a hundred forts.

3. Hence riches came to thee, the King, O sapient one: the strong-winged bird,
Unwearied, brought thee from the sky.

4. And now, sent forth, he hath attained to mighty power and majesty,
Active and ready to assist.

5. That each may see the light, the bird brought us the guard of Law, the friend
O fall, the speeder through the air.

IV Soma Pavamana

1. For food, flow onward with thy stream, cleansed and made bright by sapient men:
Indu, with sheen approach the milk!

2. While thou art cleansed, song-lover. bring comfort and vigourto the folk,
Poured, tawny one! on milk and curds!

3. Purified for feast of Gods, go thou to Indra's resting-place,
Resplendent, furthered by the strong!

V Agni.

1. By Agni Agni is inflamed, Lord of the house, wise, young,. who bears
Our gifts: the ladle is his mouth.

2. God, Agni, be his sure defence who, lord of sacrificial gifts.
Worshippeth thee the messenger.

3. Be gracious, brilliant Godl to him who, rich in sacred gifts,would fain
Call Agni to the feast of Gods!

VI Mitra Varuna

1. Mitra of holy strength I call, and foe-destroying Varuna,
Who perfect prayer with offered oil.

2. By Law, O Mitra, Varuna, Law-strengtheners who cleave to Law,
Have ye obtained your lofty power.

3. The Sages, Mitra, Varuna, of wide dominion, mighty ones,
Bestow on us effectual strength.

VII Maruts

1. So mayst thou verily be seen coming with fearless Indra: both
Of equal splendour, bringing bliss!

2. Thereafter they, as is their wont, resumed the state of new-born babes,
Taking their sacrificial name.

3. Thou, Indra, with the rapid Gods who shatter even what is firm,
Even in the cave didst find the cows.

VIII Indra-Agni

1. I call the twain whose deed wrought here hath all been famed in ancient time:
Indra and Agni harm us not!

2. The strong, the scatterers of the foe, Indra and Agni we invoke:
May they be kind to one like me:

3. Ye slay our Arya foes, O Lords of heroes, slay our Dasa foes:
Ye drive all enemies away.

IX Soma Pavamana

1. The living drops of Soma juice pour, as they flow the gladdening drink,
Intelligent drops above the station of the sea, exhilarating, dropping meath.

2. May Pavamana, King and God, speed with his wave over the sea the lofty rite!
Do thou by Mitra's and by Varuna's decree flow furthering the lofty rite:

3. Far-seeing, lovely, guided by the men, the God whose habitation is the sea!

X Soma Pavamana

1. Three are the voices that the car-steed utters: he speaks the lore of prayer, the thought of Order.
To the cows' master come the cows inquiring: the hymns with eager longing come to Soma.

2. To Soma come the cows, the milch-kine longing, to Soma sages with their hymns inquiring.
Soma, effused, is purified and lauded: our hymns and Trishtup songs unite in Soma.

3. Thus, Soma, as we pour thee into vessels, while thou art purified, flow for our welfare!
Pass into Indra. with great joy and rapture: make the voice swell, and generate abundance!

XI Indra

1. O Indra, if a hundred heavens and if a hundred earths were thine,--
No, not a hundred suns could match thee at thy birth, not both the worlds, O Thunderer.

2. Thou, hero, hast performed thy hero deeds with might, yea, all with strength, O strongest one.

Maghavan, help us to a stable full of kine, O Thunderer, with wondrous aids!

XII Indra

1. We compass thee like water, we whose grass is trimmed and Soma pressed.

Here where the filter pours its stream, thy worshippers round thee, O Vritra-slayer, sit.

2. Men, Vasu! by the Soma with lauds call thee to the foremost place.

When cometh he athirst unto the juice as home, O Indra, like a bellowing bull?

3. O valiant hero, boldly win thousandfold spoil with Kanva's sons!

O active Maghavan, with eager prayer we crave the yellowhued with store of klne.

XIII Indra

1. With Plenty for his true ally the active man will gain the spoil.

Your Indra, much-invoked, I bend with song, as bends a wright his wheel of solid wood.

2. They who bestow great riches love not paltry praise: wealth comes not to the niggard churl.

Light is the task to give, O Maghavan, to one like me on the decisive day.

XIV Soma Pavamana

1. Three several words are uttered: kine are lowing cows. who give the milk:

The tawny-hued goes bellowing on.

2. The young and sacred mothers of the holy rite have uttered praise,
Embellishing the Child of Heaven.

3. From every side, O Soma, for our profit, pour thou forth four seas.
Filled full of riches thousandfold!

XV Soma Pavamana

1. The Somas, very rich in sweets, for which the sieve is distined,
flow Effused, the source of Indra's joy: may you strong juices reach the
Gods!

2. Indu flows on for Indra's sake,-thus have the deities declared.
The Lord of Speech exerts himself, controller of all power and might.

3. Inciter of the voice of song, with thousand streams the ocean flows.
Even Soma, Lord of opulence, the friend of Indra, day by day.

XVI Soma Pavamana

1. SPREAD is thy cleansing filter, Brahmanaspati: as prince thou enterest its
limbs from every side.
The raw; whose mass bath not been heated. gains not this: they only which
are dressed, which bear, attain to it.

2. High in the seat of heaven is placed the scorcher's sieve: its, threads are
standing separate, glittering with light.
The swift ones favour him who purifieth this: with brilliancy they mount up
to the height of heaven.

3. The foremost spotted Steer bath made the Mornings shine: he bellows,
fain for war, among created things.

By his high wisdom have the mighty Sages wrought: the Fathers who behold mankind laid down the germ.

XVII Agni

1. Sing forth to him, the holy, most munificent, sublime with his refulgent glow,
To Agni, ye Upastutas

2. Worshipped with gifts, enkindled, splendid, Maghavan shall win himself heroic fame:
And will not his more plentiful benevolence come to us with abundant strength?

XVIII Indra

1. We sing this strong and wild delight of thine which conquers in the fray,
Which, Caster of the Stone! gives room and shines like gold.

2. Wherewith thou foundest shining lights for Ayu and for Manu's sake:
Now joying in this sacred grass thou bearnest forth.

3. This day too singers of the hymn praise, as of old, this might of thine:
Win thou the waters every day, thralls of the strong!

XIX Indra

1. O Indra, hear Tirschi's call, the call of him who serveth thee.
Satisfy him with wealth of kine and valient offspring! Great art thou.

2. For he, O Indra, hath produced for thee the newest gladdening song,
A hymn that springs from careful drop thought, ancient and full of sacred truth.

3. That Indra will we laud whom songs and hymns of praise have magnified.

Striving to win, we celebrate his many deeds of hero might.

BOOK III.

CHAPTER I.

I Soma Pavamana

1. Fleet as swift steeds thy cows celestial have been poured, O Pavamana, with the milk into the vat.
Sages who make thee bright, O friend whom Rishis love, have shed continuous streams from out the realm of air.

2. The beams of Pavamana, sent from earth and heaven his ensigns who is ever stedfast, travel round.
When on the sieve the golden-hued is cleansed he rests within the jars as one who seats him in his place.

3. O thou who seest all things, sovran as thou art and passing strong, thy rays encompass every form.
Pervading with thy natural powers thou flowest on, and as the whole world's Lord, O Soma, thou art King.

II Soma Pavamana

1. From heaven hath Pavamana, made, as 'twere, the marvellous thunder, and
The lofty light of all mankind.

2. The gladdening and auspicious juice of thee, O Pavamana, King!
Flows o'cr the woollen straining-cloth.

3. Thy juice, O Pavamana, sends its rays abroad fixe splendid skill,
Like lustre, all heaven's light, to see.

III Soma Pavamana

1. Impetuous, bright, have they come forth, unwearied in their speed, like bulls,
Driving the black skin far away.

2. May we attain the bridge of bliss, leaving the bridge of woe behind:
The riteless Dasa may we quell!

3. The mighty Pavamana's roar is heard as 'twere the rush of rain
The lightning-Rashes move in heaven.

4. Indu, pour out abundant food with store of cattle and of gold,
Of heroes, Soma! and of steeds!

5. Flow onward, dear to all mankind fi full the mighty heaven and earth,
As Dawn, as Surya with his beams

6. On every side, O Soma, flow round us with thy protecting stream,
As Rasa flows around the world!

IV Soma Pavamana

1. Flow on, O thou of lofty thought, flow swift in thy beloved form,
Saying, I go where dwell the Gods.

2. Preparing what is unprepared, and bringing store of food to man,
Make thou the rain descend from heaven

3. Even here is he who, swift of course, hath with the river's wave Rowed down.
From heaven upon the straining cloth.

4. With might. producing glare, the juice enters the purifying sieve,
Far-seeing, sending forth its light.

5. Inviting him from far away, and even from near at hand, the juice
For Indra is poured forth as meath.

6. In union they have sung the hymn: with stones they urge the golden-
hued,
Indu for Indra, for his drink.

V Soma Pavamana

1. The glittering maids send Sdra forth, the glorious sisters, closeallied,
Send Indu forth, their mighty Lord.

2. Pervade, O Pavamana, all our treasures with repeated light,
Pressed out, O God thyself, for Gods!

3. Pour on us, Pavamana! rain, as service and fair praise for Gods:
Pour forth unceasingly for food!

VI Agni

1. The watchful guardian of the people hath been born, Agni, the very
strong, for fresh prosperity.
With oil upon his face. with high heaven-touching flame, he shineth
splendidly, pure, for the Bharatas.

2. O Agni, the Angirasas discovered thee what time thou layest hidden,
fleeing back from wood to wood.
Thou by attrition art produced as conquering might, and men, O Angiras,
call thee the Son of Strength.

3. The men enkindle Agni in his threefold seat, ensign of sacrifice, the
earliest bousehold-priest.
With Indra and the Gods together on the grass let the wise priest sit to
complete the sacrifice!

VII Mitra-Varuna

1. This Soma hath been pressed for you, Low-strengtheners, Mitra, Varuna!
List, list ye here to this may call!

2. Both Kings who never injure aught have come to their sublimest home,
The thousand-pillared, firmly based.

3. Worshipped with fat libation. Lords of gifts, Adityas, sovran Kings,
They wait on him whose life is true.

VIII Indra

1. Armed with the bones of dead Dadhyach, Indra with unresisted. might
The nine-and-ninety Vritras slew.

2. He, searching for the horse's head that in the mountains lay concealed,
Found it in Saryandvdn lake.

3. Then straight they recognized the mystic name of the creative Steer.
There in the mansion of the Moon.

IX Indra Agni

I. As rain from out the cloud, for you, Indra and Agni, from my thought
This noblest praise hath been produced.

2. Indra and Agni, listen to the singer's call: accept his songs.
Fulfil, ye mighty Lords, his prayers!

3. Give us not up to indigence, ye heroes, Indra, Agni, nor
To Slander and reproach of men!

X Soma Pavamana

1. Gold-Hued! as one who giveth strength flow on for Gods to drink, a draught
For Vayu and the Marut host!

2. The Steer shines brightly with the Gods, dear Sage in his appointed home.
Even Pavamana unbeguiled.

3. O Pavamana, sent by prayer, roaring about thy dwelling-place,
Ascend to Vayu as Law bids!

XI Soma Pavamana

1. O Soma, Indu, every day thy friendship hath been my delight.
Many fiends follow me; help me, thou tawny-hued: pass on beyond these barriers!

2. Close to thy bosom am I. Soma, day and night draining the milk, O golden hued.
Surya himself refulgent with his glow have we, as birds, o'ertaken in his course.

XII Soma Pavamana

1. Active, while being purified, he hath assailed all enemies: They deck the Sage with holy hymns.

2. The Red hath mounted to his shrine; strong Indra hath approached the juice:
In his firm dwelling let him rest!

3. O Indu, Soma, send us now great opulence from every side:
Pour on us treasures thousandfold!

XIII Indra

1. Drink Soma, Indra Lord of bays! and let it cheer thee: the stone, like a well-guided courser,
Directed by the presser's arms bath pressed it.

2. So let the draught of joy, thy dear companion, by which, O Lord of bays, thou slayest Vritras,
Delight thee, Indra, Lord of princely treasuresl

3. Mark closely, Maghavan, the word I utter, this eulogy recited by Vasislitha:
Accept the prayers I offer at thy banquet!

XIV Indra

1. Heroes of one accord brought forth and formed for kingship
Indra who wins the victory in all encounters,
For power, in firmness, in the field, the great destroyer, fierce and exceeding strong, stalwart and full of vigour.

2. The holy sages form a ring, to view and sing unto the Ram.
Inciters, very brilliant, from all deceit, are with your chariters nigh to hear.

3. Bards joined in song to Indra so that he might drink the Soma juice.
The Lord of light, that he whose laws stand fast might aid with power and with the help he gives.

XV Indra

1. He who as sovran Lord of men moves with his chariots unrestrained,
The Vritra-slayer, conqueror of all fighting hosts, preeminents, is praised in song.

2. Honour that Indra, Puruhanman! for his aid, him in whose hand of old the fair

Sustaining bolt of thunder, mighty like the God, like Surya, was deposited!

XVI Soma Pavamana

1. The Sage of heaven whose heart is wise, when laid between both hands, with roars,
Gives us delightful powers of life.

2. He, the bright son, when born, illumed his parents who had sprung to life,
Great Son, great strengtheners of Law.

3. On, onward to a glorious home, free from all guile and dear to. men,
Flow with enjoyment to our praise!

XVII Soma Pavamana

1. For, verily, Pavamana, thou, divine! endued with brightest splendour, calling all
Creatures to immortality.

2. With whom Dadhyach Navagva opened fastened doors, by whom the sages gained their wish,
By whom they won the fame of lovely Amrita in the felicity of Gods.

XVIII Soma Pavamana

1. Soma, while filtered, with his wave flows through the long wool of the sheep,
Roaring, while purified, before the voice of song.

2. With prayers they cleanse the mighty steed, sporting in wood, above the fleece:
Our hymns, intoned, have praised him of the triple height.

3. He hath been hastened to the jars, bountiful, like an eager horse,
And, lifting up his voice, while filtered, glided on.

XIX Soma Pavamana

1. Father of holy hymns, Soma flows onward, the father of the earth, father of heaven.
Father of Agni, Surya's generator, the father who begat Indra and Vishnu.

2. Brahman of Gods, the leader of the poets, Rishi of sages, chief of savage creatures,
Falcon amid the vultures, axe of forests, over the cleansing sieve goes Soma singing.

3. He, Soma Pavamana, like a river, hath stirred the wave of voice, our songs and praises
Beholding these inferior powers, the hero, well knowing, takes his stand among the cattle.

XX Agni

I. Hither, for powerful kinship, I call Agni, him who prospers you,
Most frequent at our solemn rites.

2. That through this famed one's power he may stand by us, even as Tvasbtar comes
Unto the forms that must be shaped.

3. This Agni is the Lord supreme above all glories' mid the Gods:
May he come nigh to us with strength.

XXI Indra

1. This poured libation, Indra drink, immortal, gladdening, excellent!
Streams of the bright have flowed to thee here at the seat of holy Law.

2. When, Indra, thou dost guide thy bays, there is no better charioteer:
None hath surpassed thee in thy might, none with good steeds o'ertaken
thee.

3. Sing glory now to Indra, say to him your solemn eulogies!
The drops poured forth have made him glad: pay reverence to his noblest
might!

XII Indra

1. Indra, be pleased: drive forward, hero, striker of thy bays!
Fair, like a sage, delighting in the meath, drink of the juice for rapturous
joy.

2. O Indra, fill thy belly anew with meath that seems to flow from heaven.
The sweet-voiced raptures of this juice have come, as 'twere to heaven. to
thee.

3. Indra, victorious, Mitra-like, smote, like a Yati, Vritra dead.
As Bhrigu quelled his foes, he cleft Vala in Soma's rapturous joy.

CHAPTER II.

I Soma Pavamana

1. Winner of gold and gear and cattle flow thou on, set as impregner, Indu!
'mid the worlds of life!
Rich in brave men art thou, Soma, who winnest all: these holy singers wait
upon thee with song.

2. O Soma, thou beholdest men from every side: O Pavamana, Steer, thou
wanderest through these.
Pour out upon us wealth in treasure and in gold: may we have strength to
live among the things that be!

3. Thou passest to these worlds as sovran Lord thereof, O Indu, harnessing
thy tawny well-winged mares.
May they pour forth for thee milk and oil rich in sweets:
O Soma, let the folk abide in thy decree!

II Soma Pavamana

1. The streams of Pavamana, thine, finder of all I have been ettused,
Even as Surya's rays of light.

2. Making the light that shines from heaven thou flowest on to every form,
Soma, thou swellest like a sea.

3. Shown forth thou sendest out thy voice, O Pavamana, with a roar.
Like Surya, God, as Law commands.

III Soma Pavamana

1. Hitherward have the Somas streamed, the drops while they are purified:
When blent, in waters they are raised.

2. The milk hath run to meet them like floods rushing down a precipice:
They come to Indra, being cleansed.

3. O Soma Pavamana, thou flowest as Indra's gladdener: The men have seized and lead thee forth.

4. Thou, Indu, when, expressed by stones, thou runnest to the filter, art
Ready for Indra's high decree.

5. Victorious, to be hailed with joy, O Soma, flow delighting men,
As the supporter of mankind!

6. Flow on, best Vritra-slayer; flow meet to be hailed with joyful lauds,
pure, purifying, wonderful

7. Pure, purifying, is he called, Soma effused and full of sweets,
Slayer of sinners, dear to Gods.

IV Soma Pavamana

1. The Sage hath robed him in the sheep's wool for the banquet of the Gods,
Subduing all our enemies.

2. For he, as Pavamana, sends thousandfold riches in the shape
Of cattle to the worshippers.

3. Thou graspest all things with thy mind, and purifiest thee with thoughts:
As such, O Soma, find us fame!

4. Pour on us lofty glory, send sure riches to our liberal lords:
Bring food to those who sing thy praise!

5. As thou art cleansed, O wondrous steed, O Soma, thou hast entered, like
A pious king, into the songs,

6. He, Soma, like a courser in the floods invincible, made bright
With hands, is resting in the press.

7. Disporting, like a liberal chief, thou goest. Soma to the sieve,
Lending the laud heroic strength.

V Soma Pavamana

1. Pour on us with thy juice all kinds of corn, each sort of nourishment!
And, Soma, all felicities!

2. As thine, O Indu, is the praise, and thine what springeth from, the juice,
Seat thee on the dear sacred grass!

3. And, finding for us steeds and kine, O Soma, with thy juice flow on
Through days that fly most rapidly!

4. As one who conquers, ne'er subdued, attacks and slays the enemy,
Thus, vanquisher of thousands! flow!

VI Soma Pavamana

1. Thou, Indu, with thy streams that drop sweet juices, which were poured
for help,
Hast settled in the cleansing sieve.

2. So flow thou onward through the fleece, for Indra flow to be his drink,
Seating thee in the shrine of Law!

3. As giving room and freedom, as most sweet, pour butter forth and milk,
O Soma, for the Angirasas!

VII Agni

1. Thy glories are, like lightnings from the rainy cloud, visible, Agni, like the comings of the Dawns,
When, loosed to wander over plants and forest trees, thou crammest by thyself thy food into thy mouth.

2. When, sped and urged by wind, thou spreadest thee abroad, soon piercing through thy food according to thy will,
The hosts, who ne'er decayest, eager to consume, like men on chariots, Agni! strive on every side.

3. Agni, the Hotar-priest who fills the assembly full, waker of wisdom, chief controller of the thought-
Thee, yea, none other than thyself, doth man elect priest of the holy offering, great and small, alike.

VIII Mitra-Varuna

1. Even far and wide, O Varuna and Mitra, doth your help extend:
May I obtain your kind good-will!

2. True Gods, may we completely gain food and a dwelling place from you:
Ye Mitras, may we be your own!

3. Guard us, ye Mitras, with your guards, save us, ye skilled to save: may we
Subdue the Dasyus by ourselves!

IX Indra

I. Arising in thy might, thy jaws thou shookest Indra, having drunk
The Soma which the press had shed.

2. Indra, both world gave place to thee as thou wast fighting, when thou wast

The slayer of the Dasyu hosts.

3. From Indra, have I measured out a song eight-footed with nine parts,
Delicate, strengthening the Law.

X Indra-Agni

1. Indra and Agni, these our songs of praise have sounded forth to you:
Ye who bring blessings! drink the juice

2. Come, Indra, Agni, with those teams, desired of many, which ye have,
O heroes, for the worshipper

3. With those to his libation poured, ye heroes, Indra, Agni, come:
Come ye to drink the Soma-Julce!

XI Soma Pavamana

1. Soma, flow on exceeding bright with loud roar to the reservoirs,
Resting in wooden vats thy home!

2. Let water winning Somas flow to Indra, Vayu, Varuna,
To Vishnu and Marut host!

3. Soma, bestowing food upon our progeny, from every side
Pour on us riches thousandfold.

XII Soma Pavamana

1. Pressed out by pressers Soma goes over the fleecy backs of sheep,
Goes even as with a mare in tawny-coloured stream, goes in a sweetly-sounding stream.

2. Down to the water Soma, rich in kine, bath flowed with cows, with cows that have been milked.

They have approached the mixing-vessels as a sea: the cheerer streams for the carouse.

XIII Soma Pavamana

1. O Purifying Soma, bring to us the wondrous treasure, meet.
For lauds, that is in earth and heaven!

2. Cleansing the lives of men, thou, Steer, bellowing on the sacred grass,
Gold-hued, hast settled in thy home.

3. For ye twain, Indra, Soma, are Lords of heaven's light, Lords of the kine:
Prosper, as mighty ones, our prayers

XIV Indra

1. By men hath Indra been advanced, the Vritra-slayer, to joy and strength.
Him only we invoke for help in battles whether great or small be he our aid in deeds or might!

2. For, hero, thou art like a host, art giver of abundant spoil.
Strengthening e'en the feeble, thou aidest the sacrificer, thou givest great wealth to him who pours.

3. When war and battles are on foot, booty is offered to the bold.
Yoke thou thy wildly-rushing bays! Whom wilt thou slay, and whom enrich?
Do thou, O Indra, make us rich!

XV Indra

I. The juice of Soma thus diffused, sweet to the taste, the bright cows drink,
Who travelling in splendour close to mighty Indra's side rejoice, good in their own supremacy.

2. Craving his touch the dappled kine mingle the Soma with their milk.
The milch-kine dear to Indra send forth his death dealing thunder-bolt, good in their own supremacy.

3. With veneration, passing wise, they honour his victorious might.
They follow close his many laws to win them due preeminence, good in their own supremacy.

XVI Soma Pavamana

1. Strong, mountain-born, the stalk hath been pressed in the streams for rapturous joy.
Hawk-like he settles in his home.

2. Fair is the juice beloved of Gods, washed in the waters, pressed by men:
The milch kine sweeten it with milk

3. Then, like a steed, have they adorned the inciter for eternal life,
The meath's juice at the festival.

XVII Soma Pavamana

1. Make high and splendid glory shine hitherward, Lord of food, God, on the friend of Gods
Unclose the cask of middle air

2. Roll onward from the press, O mighty one, effused, as kings, supporter of the tribes
Pour on us rain from heaven, send us the water's flow, urging our thoughts to win the spoil!

XVIII Soma Pavamana

1. Breath of the mighty Dames, the Child, speeding the plan of sacrifice,

Surpasses all things that are dear, yea, from of old.

2. The place that is concealed hath gained a share of Trita's pressing-stones,
By the seven laws of sacrifice, even that dear place.

3. He hath sent forth unto the heights the three, in stream, as Trita's wealth:
He who is passing wise measures his pathways out.

XIX Soma Pavamana

1. Flow to the filter with thy stream, effused, to win us spoil and wealth,
Soma exceeding rich in meath for Indra, Vishnu, and the Gods

2. The hymns that know not guile, caress thee, golden-coloured, in the sieve.
As mothers, Pavamana, lick the new-born calf, as Law commands.

3. Lord of great sway, thou liftest thee above the heavens, above the earth.
Thou, of Pavamana, hast assumed thy coat of mail with majesty.

XX Soma Pavamana

1. Strong Indu, bathed in milk, flows on for Indra, Soma exciting strength, for his carousal.
He quells malignity and slays the demons, King of the homestead, he who gives us comfort.

2. Then in a stream he flows, milked out with press-stones, mingled with sweetness, through the fleecy filter--
Indu rejoicing in the love of Indra, the God who gladdens for the God's enjoyment.

3. He flows, as he is cleansed, to sacred duties, a God bedewing Gods with his own juices.

Indu hath, clothed in powers that suit the season, on the raised fleece engaged the ten swift fingers.

XXI Agni

1. O Agni, God, we kindle thee, refulgent, wasting not away,
That this more glorious fuel may send forth for thee its shine to heaven.
Bring food to those who sing thy praise!

2. To thee the splendid, Lord of light! bright! wondrous! prince of men! is brought.
Oblation with the holy verse, O Agni, bearer of our gifts! Bring food to those who sing thy praise!

3. Thou heatest both the ladles in thy mouth, O brilliant prince of men!
So fill us also in our hymns abundantly, thou Lord of Strength. Bring food to those who sing thy praise!

XXII Indra

1. Sing ye a psalm to Indra; sing a great song to the lofty Sage,
To him who maketh prayer, inspired, who loveth laud.

2. Thou, Indra, art the conqueror: thou gavest splendour to the Sun.
Maker of all things, thou art mighty and All-God.

3. Radiant with light thou wentest to the sky, the luminous realm of - heaven.
The Gods, O Indra, strove to win thy friendly love.

XXIII Indra

1. This Soma hath been pressed for thee, O Indra, bold one, mightiest, come!
May Indra vigour fill thee full, as Surya fills mid-air with rays

2. Slayer of Vritra, mount thy car! The bay steeds have been yoked by prayer.
May, with its voice, the pressing-stone draw thine attention hitherward!

3. His pair of tawny coursers bring Indra, resistless in his might.
Hither to Rishis' songs of praise and sacrifice performed by men.

BOOK IV.

CHAPTER I.

I Soma Pavamana

1. Light of the sacrifice, be pours delicious meathp most wealthy, father and begetter of the Gods.
He, gladdening, best of cheerers, juice that Indra loves, enriches with mysterious treasure earth and heaven.

2. The Lord of heaven, the vigorous and far-seeing one, flowsshouting to the beaker with his thousand streams.
Coloured like gold he rests in seats where Mitra dwells, the Steer made beautiful by rivers and by sheep.

3. As Pavamana thou flowest before the streams: thou goest on, before the hymn, before the kine.
Thou sharest mighty booty in the van of war Soma, well-armed, thou art pressed out by men who press.

II Soma Pavamana

1. Through our desire of heroes, kine, and horses, vigorous Somadrops,
Brilliant and swift, have been effused.

2. They, beautified by holy men and purified in both the hands,
Are flowing through the fleecy cloth.

3. These Soma juices shall pour forth all treasures for the worshipper,
From heaven and earth and firmament.

III Soma Pavamana

1. Flow, Soma, Indu, dear to Gods, swift through the purifying sieve,
And enter fndra in thy strength

2. As mighty food speed hitherward, Indu, as a most splendid steer:
Sit in thy place as one with power

3. The well-loved meath was made to flow, the stream of the creative juice:
The Sage drew waters to himself.

4. The mighty waters, yea, the floods accompany thee mighty one,
When thou wilt clothe thee with the milk.

5. The lake is brightened in the floods. Soma, our friend, heaven's prop and stay,
Falls on the purifying cloth.

6. The tawny Bull hath bellowed. fair as mighty Mitra to behold
He gleams and flashes with the Sun.

7. Songs, Indra, active in their might, are beautified for thee, wherewith
Thou deckest thee for rapturous joy.

8. To thee who givest ample room we pray, to win the wild delight,
That Thou mayst have exalted praise,

9. Winner of kine Indu, art thou, winner of heroes, steeds, and spoil:
Primeval soul of sacrifice.

10. Pour on us, Indu! Indra-strength with a full stream of sweetness, like
Parianya, sender of the rain!

IV Soma Pavamana

1. O Soma Pavamana, be victorious, win us high renown; And make us
better than we are!

2. Win thou the light, win heavenly light, and, Soma, all felicities;
And make us better than we are!

3. Win skilful strength and mental power! O Soma, drive away our foes;
And make us better than we are!

4. Ye purifiers, purify Soma for Indra, for his drink;
Make thou us better than we are!

5. Give us our portion in the Sun through thine own mental power and aids;
And make us better than we are!

6. Through thine own mental power and aids long may we look upon the Sun:
Make thou us better than we are!

7. Well-weaponed Soma, pour to us a stream of riches doubly great;
And make us better than we are!

8. As one victorious unsubdued in battle, pour forth wealth to us:
And make us better than we are!

9. With offerings, Pavamana! men have strengthened thee as Law commands:
Make thou us better than we are!

10. O Indu, bring us wealth in steeds brilliant and quickening all life;
And make us better than we are!

V Soma Pavamana

1. Swift runs this giver of delight, even the stream of flowing juice:
Swift runs this giver of delight.

2. The Morning knows all precious things, the Goddess knows her grace to man:
Swift runs this giver of delight.

3. We have accepted thousands from Dhvasra's and Purusbanti's hands:
Swift runs this giver of delight.

4. From whom we have accepted thus thousands and three-times ten besides:
Swift runs this giver of delight.

VI Soma Pavamana

1. Forth with his stream who gladdens best these Soma juices have been poured,
Lauded with songs for mighty strength.

2. Thou flowest to enjoy the milk, and bringest valour, being, cleansed:
Winning the spoil flow hitherward

3. And, hymned by Jamadagni, let all nourishment that kine supply,
And general praises, flow to us!

VII Agni

1. For Jatavedas, worthy of our praise, will we frame with our mind this eulogy as 'twere a car.
For good, in his assembly, is this care of ours. Let us not, in thy friendship, Agni, suffer harm!

2. We will bring fuel and prepare our sacred gifts, reminding thee at each successive holy time.
Fulfil our thoughts that we may lengthen out our lives
Let us not, in thy friendship, Agni, suffer harm!

3. May we have power to kindle thee! Fulfil our prayers in thee the Gods eat the presented sacrifice.
Bring hither the Adityas, for we long for them! Let us not, in thy friendship, Agni, suffer harm!

VIII Mitra, Varuna, Aryaman

1. Soon as the Sun hath risen I sing to you, to Mitra, Varuna,
And Aryaman who slays the foe.

2. With wealth of gold may this my song bring unmolested might; may this, Sages! obtain the sacrifice!

3. May we be thine, God Varuna, and with our princes, Mitra, thine:
May we gain food and heavenly light!

IX Indra

1. Drive all our enemies away, smite down the foes who press around,
And bring the wealth for which we long:

2. Of which the world shall know forthwith as given by thee abundantly:
Bring us the wealth for which we long:

3. O Indra, that which is concealed in strong firm place precipito us:
Bring us the wealth for which we long!

X Indra-Agni

1. Yea, ye are priests of sacrifice, winners in war and holy works
Indra and Agni, mark this well!

2. Bountiful, riders on the car, slayers of Vritra unsubdued, Indra and Agni, mark this well!

3. The men with pressing-stones have pressed this meath of yours which gives delight:
Indra and Agni, mark this well!

XI Soma Pavamana

1. For Indra girt by Maruts, flow, thou Indu, very rich in meath,
To seat thee in the place of song!

2. Sage: who know the lore of speech deck thee, the strong sustainer, well:
Men make thee bright and beautiful.

3. Let Mitra, Varuna, Aryaman drink Pavamana's juice, yea, thine.
Sage! let the Maruts drink thereof.

XII Soma Pavamana

1. Deft-handed! thou when purified liftest thy voice amid the sea.
Thou, Pavamana makest riches flow to us, yellow, abundant, much-desired.

2. Made pure, as Pavamana, in the sheep's long wool, the Steer bath bellowed in the vat.
Thou flowest, Soma Pavamana! balmed with 'milk unto the meeting-place of Gods.

XIII Soma Pavamana

1. Him here, the offspring of the sea, the ten swift fingers beautify:
With the Adityas is he seen.

2. With Indra and with Vayu he, effused, flows onward with the beams
Of Surya to the cleansing sieve.

3. Flow rich in sweets and lovely for our Bhaga, Vayu, Pushan, fair
For Mitra and for Varuna!

XIV Indra

1. With Indra splendid feasts be ours, rich in all strengthening things, wherewith,
Wealthy in food, we may rejoice!

2. Like thee, thyself, for singers yoked, thou movest, as it were besought,
Bold one, the axle of the car,

3. That, Satakratu, thou, to serve and please thy praisers, as it were,
Stirrest the axle with thy strength.

XV Indra

1. As a good cow to him who milks, we call the doer of good deeds,
To our assistance day by day.

2. Come thou to our libations, drink of Soma, Soma-drinker! yea,
The rich one's rapture giveth kine.

3. So may we be acquainted with thine innermost benevolence:
Neglect us not; come hitherward!

XVI Indra

1. As, like the Morning, thou has filled, O Indra, both the earth and heaven,
So as the mighty one, great King of all the mighty race of men, the Goddess mother brought thee forth, the blessed mother gave thee life.

2. Thou bearest in thine hand a lance like a long hook, great counsellor.
As with his foremost foot a goat, draw down the branch O Maghavan. The Goddess mother brought thee forth, the blessed mother gave thee life.

3. Relax that mortal's stubborn strength whose heart is bent on wickedness.
Trample him down beneath thy feet who watches for and aims at us. The Goddess mother brought thee forth, the blessed mother gave thee life.

XVII Soma Pavamana

1. Soma, the dweller on the hills, effused, hath flowed into the sieve.
All-bounteous art thou in carouse.

2. Thou art a holy bard, a Sage; the meath offspring of thy sap:
All bounteous art thou in carouse.

3. All-d6ties of one accorcl have come that they may drink of thee:
All-bounteous art thou in carouse.

XVIII Soma Pavamana

1. Effused is he who brings good things, who brings us store of wealth, and sweet refreshlng food,
Soma who brings us quiet homes:

2. He whom our Indra and the Marut host shall drink, Bhaga shall drink with Aryaman,
By whom we bring to us Mitra and Varuna, and Indra for our great defence.

XIX Soma Pavamana

1. Friends, hymn your Lord who makes him pure for rapturous carouse: let them
Sweeten him, as a child, with lauds and sacred gifts

2. Like as a calf with mother cows, so Indu is urged forth and sent,
Glorified by our hymns;, the god-delighting juice.

3. Effectual help to power is he. he is a banquet for the troop,
He who hath been effused, more rich in meath, for Gods.

XX Soma Pavamana

1. For us the Soma juices flow, the drops best furtherers of weal,
Effused as friends, without a spot, benevolent, finders of the light.

2. These Soma juices, skill.ed in song, purified, blent with milk and curd,
Hastening on and firmly set in oil resemble beauteous suns.

3. Effused by means of pressing- stones, upon the oxhide visible,
They, treasure-finders, have announced food unto us from every side.

XXI Soma Pavamana

1. Pour forth this wealth with this purification: flow onward to the yellow lake, O Indu!
Here, too, the bright one, wind-swift, full of wisdom, shall give a son to him who cometh quickly.

2. Flow on for us with this purification to the famed ford of thee whose due is glory!
May the foe-queller shake us down, for triumph, like a tree's ripe fruit, sixty thousand treasures!

3. Eagerly do we pray for those two exploits, at the blue lake and Prisana, wrought in battle.
He sent our enemies to sleep and slew them, and turned away the foolish and unfriendly.

XXII Agni

1. O Agni, be our nearest friend, yea, our protector and our kind deliverer!

As gracious Agni, famed for treasures, come, and, most resplendent, give us store of wealth!

2. To thee then, O most bright, O radiant God, we come with prayer for happiness for our friends.

XXIII Indra

1. May we, with Indra and the Gods to aid us, bring these existing worlds to full completion!

2. Our sacrifice, our bodies, and our offspring, let Indra with the Adityas-form and finish!

3. With the Adityas, with the band of Maruts, let Indra send us medicines to heal us!

XXIV Indra

1. Sing to your Indra, mightiest Vritra-slayer, sing to the Sage the song that he accepteth!

CHAPTER II.

I Soma Pavamana

1. The God declares the deities' generations, like Usana, proclaiming lofty wisdom.
With brilliant kin far-ruling, sanctifying, the wild boar, singing with his foot, advances.

2. The swans, the Vrishagnas from anear us, restless, have brought their clamour to our dwelling--
Friends come to Pavamana, meet for praises-and sound in concert their resistless music.

3. He takes the swiftness of the great Far strider: cows low as, 'twere to him who sports at pleasure.
He with the sharpened horns brings forth abundance: the silvery shines by night, by day the golden.

4. Like cars that thunder on their way, like coursers eager for renown,
Have Soma drops flowed forth for wealth.

5. Forth have they rushed from holding hands, like chariots that are urged to speed,
Like joyful songs of singing-men.

6. The Somas deck themselves with milk as kings are graced with eulogies,
And, with seven priests, the sacrifice.

7. Pressed for the gladdening draught the drops flow forth abundantly with song,
Flow with the stream of savoury juice.

8. Winning Vivasvan's glory and speeding the light of Dawn, the suns,
Pass through the openings of the cloth.

9. The singing-men of ancient time open the doors of sacred songs--
The men who bring the mighty One.

10. In close society have come the priests, the sevenfold brotherhood,
Filling the station of the One.

11. He makes us kin with Gods, he joins the Sun, for seeing, with mine eye;
I milk the Sage's offspring forth.

12. The Sun beholdeth with his eye the heaven's dear quarter which the priests
Have set within the sacred cell.

II Soma Pavamana

1. Forth on their way the glorious drops have flowed for maintenance of Law,
Knowing what suits this worshipper.

2. Down in the mighty waters sinks the stream of Meath, most excellent,
Oblation best of all in worth.

3. About the holy place the Steer, true, guileless, noblest, hath sent forth,
Continuous voices in the wood.

4. When the Sage, purging manly deeds and lofty wisdom flows, around,

5. When purified, he sits enthroned as King over the warring clans.
What time the sages speed him on.

6. Most dear, gold-coloured, in the fleece he sinks, and settles in the wood:

The singer is besieged with song.

7. He goes to Indra, Vayu, and the Asvins with the rapturous joy,
To whomsoe'er his power delights.

8. The waves of pleasant Soma flow to Bhaga, Mitra, Varuna,
Well knowing, through his mighty powers.

6. Gain for us, O ye Heaven and Earth, riches of Meath to win us strength:
Gain for us treasures and renown.

10. We choose to-day that chariot-steed of thine, the strong, that brings us bliss,
The guardian, the desire of all;

11. The excellent, the gladdener, the Sage with heart that understands.
The guardian, the desire of all;

12. Who for ourselves, O thou most wise, is wealth and fair intelligence,
The guardian, the desire of all.

III Agni

1. Agni Vaisvanara, born in course of Order, the messenger of earth, the head of heaven,
The Sage, the Sovran, guest of men, our vessel fit for their mouth, the Gods have generated.

2. To thee, immortal! when to life thou springest all the Gods sing for joy as to their infant.
They by thy mental powers were made immortal, Vaisvdnara when thou shonest from thy parents.

3. Him have they praised, mid-point of sacrifices, great cistern of libations, seat of riches.

Vaisvanara, conveyer of oblations, ensign of worship, have the Gods
engendered.

IV Mitra-Varuna

1. Sing forth unto your Varuna and Mitra with a song inspired:
They, mighty Lords, are lofty law.

2. Full springs of fatness, sovran Kings, Mitra and Varuna, the twain,
Gods glorified among the Gods,

3. So help ye us to riches, great celestial and terrestrial wealth!
Vast is your sway among the Gods.

V Indra

1. O Indra marvellously bright, come, these libations long for thee,
Thus by firie fingers purified!

2. Urged by the holy singer, sped by song, come nigb, O Indra, to
The sacrificing suppliant's pravers!

3. Approach, O Indra, basting thee, Lord of bay horses, to our prayers:
In our libation t ake delight!

VI Indra-Agni

1. Glorify him who compasses all forests with his glowing Dame,
And leaves them blackened by his tongue.

2. He who gains Indra's grace by fire enkindled, finds as easy way
Over the floods to splendid wealth.

3. Give us, ye twain, swift steeds to bring Indra and Agni, and bestow
Abundant food with wealth on us.

VII Soma Pavamana.

1. Indu hath started forth for Indra's settled place, and slights not,. as a friend, the promise of his friend.
Soma comes onward like a youth with youthful maids, and gains the beaker by a course of hundred paths.

2. Your hymns of pleasant sound, praiseworthy, fond of lauds, have come into the hall enclosed for sacrifice.
Singers have hymned the golden-coloured as he sports, and milchkine have come near to meet him with their milk,

3. O Soma, Indu, while they cleanse thee, with thy wave pour orb us plentiful accumulated food,
Which, ceaseless, thrice a day shall yield us hero power enriched. with store of nourishment, and strength, and meath.

VIII Indra.

1. No one by deed attains to him who works and strengthensevermore:
No, not by sacrifice, to Indra praised of all, resistless, daring, bold in might;

2. The powerful conqueror, invincible in war, him at whose birth the mighty ones,
The kine who spread afar, sent their loud voices out, heavens, earths sent their loud voices out.

IX Soma Vaisvanara

1. Sit down, O friends, and sing aloud to him who purifies himself:
Deck him for glory, like a child, with holy rites

2. Loose him who bringeth household wealth, even as a calf with. mother kine,

Him who bath double strength, strong, god-delighting juice!

3. Purify him who gives us power, most blissful one, that he may be
A banquet for the troop, Mitra, and Varuna!

X Soma Pavamana

1. The Strong hath flowed forth in a thousand streams, flowed through the filter and the sheep's long wool.

2. With ceaseless genial flow the Strong hath run, purified by the waters, blent with milk.

3. Pressed out with stones, directed by the men, go forth, O Soma, into Indra's throat!

XI Soma Pavamana

1. The Soma juices which have been expressed afar or near at hand,
Or there on Saryanavan's bank,

2. Those pressed among Arjikas, pressed among the active, in, men's homes,
Or pressed among the Fivefold Tribes--

3. May these celestial drops, expressed, pour forth upon us, as they flow,
Rain from the heavens and hero strength!

XII Agni

1. May Vatsa draw thy mind away even from thy loftiest dwelling-place!
Agni, I yearn for thee with song.

2. Thou art alike in many a place: through all the regions thou art Lord.
In fray and fight we call on thee.

3. When we are seeking spoil we call Agni to help us in the strife,
Giver of wordrous gifts in war.

XIII Indra

1, O Indra, bring great strength to us, bring valour, 5atakratu, thou most active, bring
A hero conquering in war!

2. For, gracious Satakratu, thou hast ever been a mother and a sire to us,
So now for bliss we pray to thee.

3. To thee, strong! much-invoked! who showest forth thy strength, made very mighty! do I speak:
So grant thou us heroic power!

XIV Indra

1. Stone-Darting Indra, wonderous God, what wealth thou hast not given me here,
That bounty, treasure-finder! bring, filling full both thy hands, to us!

2. Bring what thou deemest worth the wish, O Indra that which is in heavem!
So may we know thee as thou art a giver boundless in thy gifts!

3. Thy lofty spirit famed in all the regions as appeasable,--
With this thou rendest even things firm, Stone-darter! so to win thee strength.

BOOK V.

CHAPTER I.

I Soma Pavamana

1. The Maruts with their troop adorn and brighten, even at his birth, the Sage, the lovely infant.
By songs a poet, and a Sage by wisdom, Soma goes singing through the cleansing filter.

2. Light-winner, Rishi-minded, Rishi-maker, hymned in a thousand hymns, leader of sages,
Eager to gain his third form, mighty, Soma is, like Viraj, resplendent as a singer.

3. Hawk seated in the press, bird wide-extended, the banner seeking kine and wielding weapons,
Uniting with the sea, the wave of waters, the mighty tells his fourth form and declares it.

II Soma Pavamana

1. Obeying Indra's dear desire these Soma juices have flowed forth
Increasing his heroic might.

2. Laid in the press and flowing pure to Vayu and the Asvins, may
These give us great heroic strength.

3. Soma, as thou art purified, incite to bounty Indra's heart,
To seat him in the shrine of Gods!

4. The ten swift fingers deck thee forth seven ministers impel thee on,
The sages have rejoiced in thee.

5. When through the filter thou art poured we clothe thee with a robe of milk,
To be a rapturous feast for Gods.

6. When purified within the jars, Soma bright-red and golden-hued,
Hath veiled him in a milky dress.

7. Flow onward to our wealthy lords. Drive all our enemies away:
O Indu, pass into thy friend!

8. May we obtain thee, Indra's drink, who viewest men and findest light,
Gain thee and progeny and food!

9. Send down the rain from heaven and make splendour upon the earth!
Give us,
O Soma, victory in war!

III Soma Pavamana

1. Poured through the fleece in thousand streams purified Soma floweth to,
Indra's and Vayu's meeting-place.

2. Sing forth, ye men who long for help, to Pavamana, to the Sage,
Effused to entertain the Gods!

3. The Soma drops with thousand powers are purified to win us strength,
Hymned to become the feast of Gods.

4. Yea, as thou flowest bring great store of food that we may win us strength:
Indu, bring splendid manly might

5. Like coursers by their drivers urged, they were poured forth, to win us strength,
Swift through the woollen straining-cloth.

6. May they in flowing give us wealth in thousands, and heroic power,--
These godlike Soma drops effused!

7. The roaring Soma drops flow on, like milch-kine lowing to, their calves:
They have run forth from both the hands.

8. Beloved by Indra, bringing joy, roaring as thou art purified,
Drive all our enemies away.

9. As Pavamanas, driving off the godless, looking on the light,
Sit in the place of sacrifice.

IV Soma Pavamana

1. The Soma drops, exceeding rich in sweets, to Indra have been poured,
Shed with the stream of sacrifice.

2. Sages have called to Indra, like cows, milch-kine, lowing to their calves,
Called him to drink the Soma juice.

3. In the stream's wave wise Soma dwells, distilling rapture, in his. seat,
Resting upon a wild cow's hide.

4. Far-sighted Soma, Sage and bard, is worshipped in the central point,
Of heaven, the straining-cloth of wool.

5. In close embracement Indu holds Soma when poured within the: jars.
And on the purifying sieve.

6. Indu sends forth a voice on high, up in the region of the sea.
Stirring the cask that drops with meath.

7. The tree whose praises never fail dwells in the stream of holy milk,
Urged onward by its human friend.

8. O Pavamana bring us wealth bright with a thousand splendours; yea,
O Indu, give us ready help!

9. Sage, poet, poured with all his stream, Soma is driven, far away,
To the dear places of the sky.

V Soma Pavamana

1. Loud as a river's roaring wave thy powers have lifted up themselves:
Urge on thine arrow's sharpened point!

2. At thine effusion upward rise three voices fresh and strong, when thou.
Flowest upon the fleecy ridge.

3. On to the fleece they urge with stones the dear, the goldencoloured one,
Even Pavamana dropping meath.

4. Flow with thy current to the sieve, O Sage, best giver of delight,
To seat these in the shrine of song!

5. Best giver of delight, flow on anointed with the milk for balm,
And enter into Indra's throat!

VI Soma Pavamana

1. Flow onward, Indu, with this food for him who in thy wild delights,
Battered the nine-and-ninety down.

2. Smote swiftly forts, and Sambara, then Yadu and that Turvasa,
For pious Divodasa's sake!

3. Finder of horses, pour on us horses and wealth in kine and gold,
And Indu, food in boundless store!

VII Soma Pavamana

1. Chasing our foemen, driving off the godless, Soma floweth on,
Going to Indra's settled place.

2. O Pavamana, hither bring great riches, and destroy our foes:
O Indu, grant heroic fame!

3. A hundred obstacles have ne'er checked thee when rain to give thy boons,
When, being cleansed, thou combatest.

VIII Soma Pavamana

1. Flow onward with that stream wherewith thou gavest splendour to the sun,
Speeding the waters kind to man!

2. He, Pavamana, high o'er man, yoked the Sun's courser Etasa,
To travel through the realm of air.

3. Yea, those bay steeds he harnessed to the chariot that the Sun might come:
Indu, he said, is Indra's self.

IX Agni

1. Associate with fires, make your God Agni envoy at sacrifice, best skilled in worship,
Established firm among mankind, the holy flame-crowned and fed with oil, the purifier!

2. Like a steed neighing eager for the pasture, when he hath stepped forth from the great enclosure:
Then the wind following blows upon his splendour, and, straight, the path is black which thou hast travelled.

3. From thee, a bull but newly born, O Agni, the kindled everlasting flames rise upward.
Aloft to heaven as ruddy smoke thou mountest: Agni, thou speedest to the Gods as envoy.

X Indra

1. We make this Indra very strong to strike the mighty Vritra dead:
A vigorous hero shall he be.

2. This Indra, made for giving gifts, is stablished, mightiest, in strength,
Bright, meet for Soma, famed in song.

3. By song, as 'twere' the powerful bolt which none may parry, was prepared:
Strong and invincible he grew.

XI Soma Pavamana

I. Adhvaryu, to the filter lead the Soma-juice expressed with stones:
Make thou it pure for Indra's drink!

2. These Gods and all the Marut host, Indu! enjoy this juice of thine,
This Pavamana's flowing meath.

3. Pour out for Indra, Thunder-armed, the milk of heaven, the Soma's juice,
Most excellent, most rich in sweets!

XII Soma Pavamana

1. On flows the potent juice, sustainer of the heavens, the strength of Gods, whom men must hail with shouts of joy,
Thou, gold-hued, started like a courser by brave men, art lightly showing forth thy splendour in the streams.

2. He takes his weapons, like a hero, in his hands, fain to win light, car-borne, in forays for the kine.
Indu, while stimulating Indra's might, is urged forward and balmed by sages skilful in their task.

3. Soma, as thou art purified with flowing wave, exhibiting thy strength enter thou Indra's throat.
Make both worlds stream for us, as lightning doth the clouds: mete out exhaustless powers for us through this our prayer!

XIII Indra

1. Though, Indra, thou art called by men eastward and westward, north and south,
Thou chiefly art with Anava and Turvasa, brave champion! urged by men to come.

2. Or, Indra, when with Ruma, Rusama, Syavaka, and Kripa thou rejoicest thee,
Still do the Kanvas, bringing prayer, with hymns of praise O Indra, draw thee hither: come!

XIV Indra

1. Both boons,-may, Indra, hitherward turned, listen to this prayer of ours.
And mightiest Maghavan with thought inclined to us come near to drink to Soma juice!

2. For him, strong, independent ruler, Heaven and Earth have fashioned forth with power and might.

Thou seatest thee as first among thy peers in place, for thy soul longs for Soma juice.

XV Soma Pavamana

1. God, working with mankind flow on; to Indra go thy gladdening juice:
To Vayu mount as Law commands!

2. O Soma Pavamana, thou pourest out wealth that may be famed:
O Indu, pass into the lake!

3. Soma, thou flowest chasing foes, finder of wisdom and delight:
Drive thou the godless folk afar!

XVI Soma Pavamana

1. Stream on us riches that are craved by hundreds, best at winning spoil,
Riches, O Indu, thousandfold, most splendid, that surpass the light!

2. May we, O Vasu, be most near to this thy bounty, food, and wealth!
Desired by many men, and in thy favour, O resistless one!

3. Effused, this Indu hath flowed on, distilling rapture, to the fleece.
He streams erect to sacrifice, as 'twere with splendour, seeking kine.

XVII Soma Pavamana

1. Flow onward, Soma, as a mighty sea, as Father of the Gods, to every form!

2. Flow on, O Soma, radiant for the Gods, blissful to heaven and earth and living things!

3. Thou art, bright juice, sustainer of the sky: flow, mighty, in accordance with true law!

XVIII Agni

I. I laud your most beloved guest, like a dear friend,
O Agni, him!
Who, like a chariot, wins us wealth.

2. Whom as a Sage who merits praise the Gods have, from the olden time,
Established among mortal men.

3. Do thou, most youthful God, protect the men who offer, hear their songs,
And of thyself preserve their seed!

XIX Indra

1. Come unto us, O Indra, dear, still conquering, unconcealable
Wide as a mountain spread on all sides, Lord of heaven.

2. O truthful Soma-drinker, thou art mightier than both the worlds.
Thou strengthenest him who pours'libation, Lord of heaven.

3. For thou art he, O Indra, who upholdeth all our fortresses,
The Dasyu's slayer, man's sustainer, Lord of heaven.

XX Indra

1. Render of forts, the young, the wise, of strength unmeasured, was he born,
Sustainer of each sacred rite, Indra, the Thunderer, much extolled,

2. Thou wielder of the stone, didst burst the cave of Vala rich in kine.
The Gods came pressing to thy side, and free from terror aided thee.

3. They glorified with hymns of praise Indra who reigneth by his might,

Whose bounteous gifts in thousands come, yea, even more abundantly.

CHAPTER II.

I Soma Pavamana

1. Guard of all being, generating creatures, loud roared the sea as highest law commanded.
Strong in the filter, on the fleecy summit, pressed from the stone, Soma hath waxen mighty.

2. Make Vayu glad, for furtherance and bounty: cheer Varuna and Mitra, as they cleanse thee!
Gladden the Gods, gladden the host of Maruts: make Heaven and Earth rejoice, O God, O Soma!

3. Soma, the mighty, when, the water's offspring, he chose the Gods, performed that great achievement.
He, Pavamana, granted strength to Indra: he, Indu, generated strength in Surya.

II Soma Pavamana

1. Here present this immortal God flies, like a bird upon her wings,
To settle in the vats of wood.

2. Praised by the sacred bards, this God dives into waters, and bestows
Rich gifts upon the worshipper.

3. He. like a warrior going forth with heroes, as he flows along.
Is fain to win all precious boons.

4. This God as he is flowirig on speeds like a car and gives his aid:
He lets his voice be heard of all.

5. This God, while flowing, is adorned, gold-coloured, for the spoil, by men
Devout and skilled in holy songs.

6. This God, made ready with the hymn runs swiftly through the winding
ways,
Inviolable as he flows.

7. A way he rushes with his stream, across the regions, into heaven,
And roars as he is flowing on.

8. While flowing, meet for sacrifice, he hath gone up to heaven, across
The regions, never overthrown.

9. By generation long ago, this God, engendered for the Gods,
Flows tawny to the straining-cloth.

10. This Lord of many holy laws, even at his birth engendering strength,
Effused, flows onward in a stream.

III Soma Pavamana

1. Through the fine fingers, with the song, this hero comes with rapid cars,
Going to Indra's settled place.

2. In holy thought he ponders much for the great service of theGods,
Where the immortals have their seat.

3. Men beautify him in the vats, him worthy to be beautified,
Him who brings forth abundant food.

4. He is deposited and led along the consecrated path
When zealous men are urging him,

5. He moves, a vigorous steed, adorned with beauteous rays of shining gold,
He who is Sovran of the streams.

6. He brandishes his horns on high, and whets them, bull who leads the herd,
Doing with might heroic deeds.

7. He, over places rough to pass bringing rich treasures, closely pressed.
Descends into the reservoirs.

8. Him, even him the golden-hued, well armed, best giver of delight,
Ten fingers urge to run his course.

IV Soma Pavamana

1. This Bull, this chariot robes him in the sheep's long wool as heproceeds.
To war that wins a thousand spoils.

2. The dames of Trita with the stones urge forth this goldencoloured one,
Indu to Indra for his drink.

3. He like a falcon settles down amid the families of men,
Like lover speeding to his love.

4. This young exhilarating juice looks downward from its place in heaven,
This Soma drop that pierced the sieve.

5. Pressed for the draught, this tawny juice flows forth intelligent, calling out,
Unto the well-beloved place.

6. Him, here, the gold-decked skilful ten cleanse carefully, who make him bright.
And beauteous for the gladdening draught.

V Soma Pavamana

1. Urged by the men, this vigorous steed, Lord of the mind omniscient,
Flies to the long wool of the sheep.

2. Within the filter hath he flowed, this Soma for the Gods effused.
Entering all their essences.

3. He shines in beauty there, this God, immortal, in his dwellingplace,
Foe-slayer, dearest to the Gods.

4. Directed by the sisters ten, bellowing on his way this Steer
Runs onward to the wooden vats.

5. This Pavamana, gladdening drink within the purifying sieve,
Gave splendour to the Sun in heaven.

6. Unconquerable Lord of speech, dwelling beside Viavasvan, he
Mounts up together with the Sun.

VI Soma Pavamana

1. This Sage, exalted by our lands, flows to the purifying sieve,
Scattering foes as he is cleansed.

2. Giver of strength, winner of light, for Indra and for Vayu he
Is poured upon the filtering-cloth.

3. The men conduct him, Soma, Steer, omniscient the head of heaven.
Effused into the vats of wood.

4. Longing for kine, longing for gold hath Indu Pavamana roared,
Still conqueror, never overcome.

5. To Indra in the firmament this mighty tawny Steer hath flowed
This Indu, being purified.

6. This Soma being purified flows mighty and invincible, Slayer of sinners,
dear to Gods.

VII Soma Pavamana

1. This Soma, strong effused for draught, flows to the purifying sieve,
Slaying the fiends, loving the Gods.

2. Far sighted, tawny-coloured, he flows to the sieve intelligent,
Bellowing to his place of rest.

3. This vigorous Pavamana runs forth to the luminous realm of heaven,
Fiend-slayer, through the sheep's long wool.

4. This Pavamana, up above on Trita's ridge, hath made the Sun,
Together with the Sisters, shine.

5. Effused, this Soma, Steer, who slays Vritra, room-giver, unbeguiled,
Hath gone as 'twere to win the spoil.

6. Urged by the sage upon his way, this God speeds forward to the: vats,
Indu to Indra, giving boons.

VIII Soma Pavamana

1. The man who reads the essence stored by saints, the Pavamana hymns,
Tastes food completely purified, made sweet by Matarisvan's touch.

2. Whoever reads the essence stored by saints, the Pavamana hymns,
For him Sarasvat! pours forth water and butter, milk and meath.

3. Yea, for the Pavamanas flow richly, drop fatness, bring us weal,--

Amrit deposited among the Brahmans, essence stored by saints.

4. So may the Pavamana hymns bestow on us this world and that,
And gratify our hearts' desires'-the Goddesses combined with Gods!

5. The purifying flood wherewith Gods ever purify themselves,--
With that, in thousand currents, may the Pavamanas make us clean!

6. The Pavamana hymns bring weal: by these man goes to Paradise,
And, eating pure and holy food, attains to immortality.

IX Agni

1. We with great reverence have approached the Youngest, who hath shone forth well kindled in his dwelling,
Wondrously bright between wide earth and heaven, well worshipped, looking forth in all directions.

2. Through his great might o'ercoming all misfortunes, praised in the house is Agni Jatavedas.
May he preserve us from disgrace and trouble, both us who laud him and our wealthy princes!

3. O Agni, thou art Varuna and Mitra: Vasishthas! with their holy hymns exalt thee.
With thee be most abundant gain of treasure!
Do ye preserve us evermore with blessing!

X Indra

1. Indra, great in his power and might, and like Parjanya rich in rain.
Hath been increased by Vatsa's lauds.

2. Since Kanvas have with lauds made him completer of the sacrifice,
Words are their own appropriate arms.

3. When priests who magnify the Son of holy law present their gifts,
Sages with Order's hymn of praise.

XI Soma Pavamana

1. Of gold-hued Pavamana, great destroyer, radiant streams have flowed,
Swift streams of him whose gleams are swift.

2. Best rider of the chariot, praised with fairest praise 'mid beauteous ones,
Gold gleaming with the Marut host,

3. Penetrate, Pavamana, best at winning booty, with thy rays,
Giving the Singer hero strength!

XII Soma Pavamana

1. Hence sprinkle forth the juice effused, Soma, the best of sacred gifts,
Who, friend of man, hath run among the water-streams He hath pressed
Soma out with stones.

2. Now, being purified, flow hither through the fleece, invincible and more
odorous!
We joy in thee in waters when thou art effused, blending thee still with
juice and milk.

3. Pressed out for all to see, delighting Gods, Indu, far-seeing one, is mental
power.

XIII Soma Pavamana

1. Even as a King hath Soma, red and tawny Bull, been pressed the
wondrous one hath bellowed to the kine.
While purified thou passest through the filtering fleece to seat thee hawk-
like in the place that drops with oil.

2. Parjanya is the sire of the leaf-bearing Bull: on mountains, in earth's centre hath he made his home.
The waters have flowed forth, the Sisters, to the kine: he meets the pressing-stones at the beloved rite.

3. To glory goest thou, a Sage with ordering skill, like a groomed steed thou rushest forward to the prize.
Be gracious to us, Soma, driving off distress! Thou goest, clothed in butter, to a robe of state.

XIV Indra

1. Turning as 'twere to meet the Sun, enjoy from Indra all good things!
When he who will be born is born with power we look to treasures as our heritage.

2. Praise him who sends us wealth, prompt with his liberal boons Good 4re the gifts that Indra gives.
He is not wroth with one who satisfies his wish: he instigates, his mind to give.

XV Indra

1. Indra, give us security from that whereof we are afraid
Help us, O Maghavan, let thy favour aid us thus drive away foes and enemies!

2. For thou, O liberal Lord of ample bounty, art the ruler of our house and home.
So, Indra Maghavan, thou lover of the song, we with pressed Soma call on thee.

XVI Soma Pavamana

1. Thou, Soma, hast a running stream, sweet-toned most strong at sacrifice:
Flow bounteously bestowing wealth

2. Thou most delightful, when effused, running, the best of gladdeners, art
Indu, still conquering, ne'er subdued.

3. Do thou, poured forth by pressing- stones, flow hither uttering a roar,
And bring us brightly-glorious strength!

XVII Soma Pavamana

1. In might, O Indu, with thy streams flow for the banquet of the Gods:
Rich in meath, Soma, in our beaker take thy seat!

2. Thy drops that swim in water have exalted Indra to delight
The Gods have drunk thee up for immortality.

3. Stream opulence to us, ye drops of Soma, pressed and purified
Pouring down rain from heaven in floods, and finding light!

XVIII Soma Pavamana

1. Him with the fleece they purify, brown, golden-hued beloved of all,
Who with exhilarating juice goes forth to all the deities

2. Whom, bright with native splendour, crushed between the preesing-
stones, a friend.
Whom Indra dearly loves, the waves and ten companions dip and bathe

3. For Vritra-slaying Indra, thou, Soma, art poured that he may drink,
And for the guerdon-giving man, the hero sitting in his seat.

XIX Soma Pavamana

1. Flow onward Soma, flow for mighty strength, as a strong courser, bathed, to win the prize.

2. The pressers clarify this juice of thine, the Soma for delight and lofty fame.

3. They deck the gold-hued infant, newly-born, even Soma, Indu, in the sieve, for Gods.

XX Soma Pavamana

1. The Gods have come to Indu well-descended, beautified with milk,
The active crusher of the foe.

2. Even as mother cows their calf, so let our praise-songs strengthen him,
Yea, him who winneth Indra's heart!

3. Soma, pour blessings on our kine, pour forth the food that streams with milk:
Increase the sea, praiseworthy one!

XXI Indra

1. Hitherward! they who light the flame and straightway trim the sacred grass,
Whose friend is Indra ever young.

2. Large is their fuel, much their laud, wide is their splinter from the stake,
Whose friend is Indra ever young.

3. Unquelled in fight the hero leads his army with the warrior chiefs,
Whose friend is Indra ever young.

XXII Indra

1. He who alone bestoweth wealth on mortal man who offereth gifts,
Is Indra only, potent Lord whom none resist.

2. Whoever with the Soma pressed draws thee away from many men,-
Verily Indra gains thereby tremendous power.

3. When willhe trample, like a weed, the man who hath no gift for him?
When, verily, will Indra hear our songs of praise?

XXIII Indra

1. The singers hymn thee, they who chant the psalm of praise are lauding thee.
The Brahmans have exalted thee, O Satakratu, like a pole.

2, When thou wast climbing ridge from ridge, he looked upon the toilsome task:
Indra takes notice of that wish, and the Ram hastens with his troop.

3. Harness thy pair of strong bay steeds, long-maned, whose bodies fill the girths.
And, Indra, Soma drinker, come to listen to our songs Of praise!

BOOK VI.

CHAPTER I.

I Agni

1. Agni,well kindled bring the Gods for him who offers holy gifts;
And worship them, pure Hotar-priest!

2. O Sage, Tanunapat, present our sacrifice to Gods to-day,
Sweet to the taste, that they may help!

3. Dear Narasansa, sweet of tongue, presenter of oblations, I
Invoke to this our sacrifice.

4. Agni, on thy most easy car, entreated, hither bring the Gods!
Manus-appointed Priest art thou.

II Adityas

1. So when the Sun hath risen to-day may sinless Mitra, Aryaman, Bhaga, and Savitar send us forth!

2. May this our home be guarded well: forward, ye bounteous, on the way, Who bear us safely o'er distress!

3. Yea, Aditi, and those great Kings whose statute is inviolate, Are sovrans of a vast domain.

III Indra

1. Let Soma juices make thee glad! Display thy bounty, Thunderer: Drive off the enemies of prayer!

2. Crush with thy foot the niggard churls who bring no gifts! mighty art thou:

There is not one to equal thee.

3. Thou art the Lord of Somas pressed, Somas unpressed are also thine:

Thou art the Sovran of the folk.

IV Soma Pavamana

1. True object of our hymns, Sage, watchful Soma hath settled in the press as they refine him.

Him the Adhvaryus, paired and eager, follow, leaders of sacrifice and skilful-handed.

2. He, purified and bringing gifts to Surya, hath filled full heaven and earth, and hath disclosed them.

He by whose dear help heroes gain their wishes will yield the precious meed as to a victor.

3. He, being cleansed, the strengthener and increaser, bountiful Soma helped us his lustre,

Wherein our sires of old who knew the footsteps found light and sought the kine within the mountain.

V Indra

1. Glorify naught besides, O friends, so shall no sorrow trouble you!

Praise only mighty Indra, when the juice is shed, and say your lauds repeatedly!

2. Even him, the swift one, like a bull who rushes down men's conqueror, bounteous like a cow;

Him who is cause of both, of enmity and peace, to both sides most munificent.

VI Indra

1. These songs of our exceeding sweet, these hymns of praise ascend to thee,
Like ever-conquering chariots that display their strength, gain wealth and give unfailing help.

2. The Bhrigus are like suns, like Kanvas, and have gained each thing whereon their thought was bent.
The living men of Priyamedha's race have sun g exalting Indra with their lauds.

VII Soma Pavamana

1. Run forth to battle conquering the Vritras! thou Speedest to quell the foe like one exacting debts.

2. Thou Pavamana, didst beget the Sun with might, and rain in the supporting sky,
Hasting to us with plenty vivified with milk.

3. For, Soma, we rejoice ourselves in thee effused for great supremacy in fight;
Thou, Pavamana, enterest into mighty deeds.

VIII Soma Pavamana

1. Flow forth, O Soma, flow thou onward, sweet to Indra's,
Mitra's, Pushan's, Bhaga's taste!

2. So flow thou on as bright celestial juice, flow to the vast immortal dwelling-place!

3. Let Indra drink, O Soma, of thy juice for wisdom, and all deities for strength!

IX Soma Pavamana

1. Even as the beams of Surya, urging men to speed, they issue forth together, gladdening as they flow,
These swift outpourings in long course of holy rites: no form save only Indra shows itself so pure.

2. The thought is deeply fixed, the savoury juice is shed; the tongue with joyous sound is stirring in the mouth:
And Pavamana, like the shout of those who press, the drop, rich in sweet juice, is flowing through the fleece.

3. The bull is bellowing; the cows are coming nigh: the Goddesses approach the God's own resting-place.
Onward hath Soma pressed through the sheep's fair bright fleece, and hath, as 'twere, endued a garment newly washed.

X Agni

1. From the two fire-sticks have the men engendered, with thought, urged by the hand, the glorious Agni,
Far-seen, with pointed flame, Lord of the Homestead.

2. The Vasus set that Agni in the dwelling, fair to behold, for help, from every quarter:
Who, in the house for ever, must be honoured.

3. Shine thou before us, Agni, well-enkindled, with flame, most youthful God, that never fadeth!
To thee come goods and treasures all together.

XI Surya

1. This spotted Bull hath come and sat before the mother in the east,

Advancing to his father heaven.

2. As expiration from his breath, his radiance penetrates within
The Bull shines out through all the sky.

3. Song is bestowed upon the Bird: it reigns supreme through thirty realms.
Throughout the days at break of morn.

CHAPTER II.

I Agni

1. Chant we a hymn to Agni while we go to sacrifice, to him
Who hears us even from afar!

2. Who from of old, in carnage, when the folk were gathered, hath preserved.
His household for the worshipper.

3. May that most blissful Agni guard our wealth and all ourfamily.
And keep us safe from pain and grief

4. Yea, let men say, Agni is born, even he who slayeth Vritra, he,
Who winneth wealth in every fight!

II Agni

1. Harness, O Agni, O thou God, thy steeds which are most excellent!
The fleet ones bring the rapidly.

2. Come hither, bring the Gods to us to taste the sacrificial feast,
To drink the draught of Soma juice!

3. O Agni of the Bharatas, flame splendid with unfading might
Shine forth and gleam, eternal one!

III Soma Pavamana

1. Let him, as mortal, crave this speech for him who presses of the juice!
As Bhrigu's sons chased Makha, so drive ye the niggard hound away.

2. The kinsman hath endued his robe even as a son is clasped in arms.
He went, as lover to a dame, to take his station suitor-like.

3. That hero who produces strength, he who hath propped both worlds apart,
Gold-hued, hath wrapped him in the sieve to settle, priest-like, in his place.

IV Indra

1. Still, Indra, from all ancient time rivalless ever and companionless art thou:
Thou seekest friendship but in war.

2. Thou findest not the wealthy man to be thy friend: those scorn thee who are flown with wine.
What time thou thunderest and gatherest, then thou, even as a father, art invoked.

V Indra

1. A thousand and a hundred steeds are harnessed to thy golden car:
Yoked by devotion, Indra, let the long-maned bays bring thee to drink the Soma juice!

2. Yoked to thy chariot wrought of gold, may thy two bays with, peacock tails.
Convey thee hither, steeds with their white backs, to quaff sweet juice that makes us eloquent!

3. So drink, thou lover of the song, as the first drinker, of this juice.
This the outpouring of the savoury sap prepared is good and meet to gladden thee.

VI Soma Pavamana

1. Press ye and pour him, like a steed, laud-worthy, speeding through the region and the flood,
Who swims in water, dwells in wood

2. The Steer with thousand streams who poureth out the rain, dear to the race of deities;
Who, born in Law, hath waxen mighty by the Law, King, God, and lofty ordinance.

VII Agni

1. Served with oblation, kindled, bright, through love of song, may Agni, bent
On riches, smite the Vritras dead

2. His father's father, shining in his mother's ever-lasting side,
Set on the seat of sacrifice!

3. O active Jatavedas, bring devotion that wins progeny, Agni, that it may shine to heaven!

VIII Soma Pavamana

1. Made pure by this man's urgent zeal and impulse, the God hath with his juice the Gods pervaded.
Pressed, singing, to the sieve he goes, as passes the Hotar to enclosures hoiding cattle.

2. Robed in fair raiment meet to wear in combat, a mighty Sage pronouncing invocations,
Roll onward to the press-boards as they cleanse thee, far-seeing at the feast of Gods and watchful!

3. Dear, he is brightened on the fleecy summit, a prince among us, nobler than the noble.
Roar out as thou art purified, run forward! Do ye preserve us evermore with blessings!

IX Indra

1. Come now and let us glorify pure Indra with pure Sama hymn!
Let milk-blent juice delight him made stronger with pure, pure songs of praise!

2. O Indra, come thou pure to us, with pure assistance pure thyself!
Pure, send thou riches down to us, and, meet for Soma! pure, rejoice!

3. O Indra, pure, vouchsafe us wealth, and, pure enrich the worshipper!
Pure, thou dost strike the Vritras dead, and strivest pure, to win the spoil.

X Agni

1. Eager for wealth we meditate Agni's effectual laud to-day,
Laud of the God who touches heaven.

2. May Agni who is Hotar-priest among mankind accept our songs,
And worship the celestial folk!

3. Thou, Agni, art spread widely forth, Priest dear and excellent through thee
Men make the sacrifice complete.

XI Soma Pavamana

1. To him, praiseworthy, sacred tones have sounded, Steer of the triple height, the life-bestower.
Dwelling in wood, like Varuna, a river, lavishing treasure, he distributes blessings.

2. Great conqueror, warrior girt, Lord of all heroes, flow on thy way as he who winneth riches:
With sharpened arms, with swift bow, never vanquished in battle, vanquishing in fight the foemen!

3. Giving security, Lord of wide dominion, send us both heaven and earth with all their fulness!
Striving to win the Dawns, the light, the waters, and cattle, call to us abundant booty!

XII Indra

1. O Indra, thou art far-renowned, impetuous Lord of power and might.
Alone, the never-conquered guardian of mankind, thou smitest down resistless foes.

2. As such we seek thee now, O Asura, the most wise, craving thy bounty as our share
Thy sheltering defence is like an ample cloak. So may thy favours reach to us.

XIII Agni

1. Thee have we chosen, skilfullest in sacrifice, immortal, Priest, among the Gods,
Best finisher of this holy rite:

2. The Waters' Child, the blessed brightly-shining one, Agni whose, light is excellent.
May he by sacrifice win us in heaven the grace of Mitra, Varuna, and the Floods!

XIV Agni

1. Lord of all food is he, the man whom thou protectest in the fight,
Agni, and urgest to the fray.

2. Him, whosoever he may be, no one may vanquish, mighty one!
Nay, very glorious wealth is his.

3. May he who dwells with all mankind conquer in fight with steeds of war,
With sages may he win the spoil.

XV Soma Pavamana

1. Ten sisters, pouring out the rain together, the sage's quickly
moving thoughts, adorn him.
Hither hath run the gold-hued Child of Surya, and reached the vat like a
fleet vigorous courser.

2. Even as a youngling shouting with his mothers, the bounteous Steer hath
flowed along with waters.
As youth to damsel, so with milk he hastens on to the settled meeting-
place, the beaker.

3. Yea, swollen is the udder of the milch-cow; thither in streams. comes
very sapient Indu.
The kine make ready, as with new-washed treasures, the head and chief
with milk within the vessels.

XVI Indra

1. Drink, Indra, of the savoury juice, and cheer thee, with our milky
draught!
Be, for our weal, our friend and sharer of the feast, and let thy wisdom
guard us well!

2. In thy kind grace and favour may we still be strong: cast us not down
before the foe!

With manifold assistance guard and succour us, and stablish us in thy good-will!

XVII Soma Pavamana

1. The three-times seven milch-kine in the loftiest heaven have for this Soma poured the genuine milky draught.
Four other beauteous creatures hath he made for his adornment when he waxed in strength through holy rites.

2. Enjoying lovely Amrit by his wisdom he divided, each apart from other, earth and heaven.
He gladly wrapped himself in the most lucid floods, when through their glory they-found the God's resting-place.

3. May those his brilliant rays be ever free from death, inviolate for both classes of created things--
Rays wherewith powers of men and Gods are purified! Yea, even for this have sages welcomed him as King.

XVIII Soma Pavamana

1. Lauded with song, to feast him, flow to Vayu, flow purified to Varuna and Mitra!
Flow to the song inspiring car-borne hero, to mighty Indra, him who wields the thunder!

2. Pour on us garments that shall clothe us meetly, send, purified, milch-kine, abundant yielders!
God Soma, send us cbariot-drawing horses that they may bring us treasures bright and golden!

3. Send to us in a stream celestial riches, send us when thou art cleansed, what earth containeth,

So that thereby we may acquire possessions and Rishihood in Jamadagni's manner!

XIX Indra

1. When thou, unequalled Maghavan, wast born to smite the Vritras dead,
Thou spreadest out the spacious earth and didst support and prop the heavens.

2. Then was the sacrifice produced for thee, the laud, and song of joy.
In might thou art above this All, all that now is and yet shall be.

3. Raw kine thou filledst with ripe milk. Thou madest Surya rise to heaven.
Heat him as milk is heated with pure Sdma hymns, great joy to him who loves the song!

XX Indra

1. Rejoice: thy glory hath been quaffed, Lord of bay steeds! as 'twere the bowl's enlivening mead.
Thine, Steer, is Indu, Steer, the Strong, best winner of a thousand spoils.

2. Let our strong drink, most excellent, exhilarating, come to thee,
Victorious, Indra! bringing gain, immortal conquering in fight!

3. Thou, hero, winner of the spoil, urgest to speed the car of man.
Burn, like a vessel with the flame, the riteless Dasyu, conqueror!

CHAPTER III.

I Soma Pavamana

1. Pour down the rain upon us, pour a wave of waters from the sky.
And plenteous store of wholesome foood!

2. Flow onward with that stream of thine, whereby the cows have come to us.
The kine of strangers to our home.

3. Dearest to Gods in sacred rites, pour on us fatness with thy stream,
Pour down on us a flood of rain!

4. To give as vigour, with thy stream run through the fleecy straining-cloth!
For verily the Gods will hear.

5. Onward hath Pavamana flowed and beaten off the Rakshasas.
Flashing out splendour as of old.

II Indra

1. Bring forth oblations to the God who knoweth all, who fain would drink.
The wanderer, lagging not behind the hero, coming nigh with, speed!

2. With Somas go ye nigh to him chief drinker of the Soma's. juice:
With beakers to the impetuous God, to Indra with the flowing, drops!

3. What time with Somas, with the drops effused,, ye come beforethe God,
Full wise, he knows the hope of each, and, bold one strikes this. foe and that.

4. To him, Adhvaryu! yea, to him give offerings of the juiceexpressed!
Will he not keep us safely from the spiteful curse of each, presumptuous
high-born foe?

III Soma Pavamana

1. Sing ye a song to Soma brown of hue, of independent might,
The Red, who reaches up to heaven!

2. Purify Soma when effused with stones which hands move rapidly,
And pour the sweet milk in the meath.

3. With humble homage draw ye nigh; blend the libation with the curds:
To Indra offer Indu up

4. Soma, foe-queller, strong and swift, doing the will of Gods, pour forth,
Prosperity upon our kine

5. Heart-knower, Sovran of the heart, thou art effused, O Soma, Tthat,
Indra. may drink thee and rejoice.

6. O Soma Pavamana, give us riches and heroic strength, Indu, with Indra.
our ally!

IV Indra

I. Surya, thou mountest up to meet the hero famous for his wealth,
Who hurls the bolt and works for men;

2. Him who with might of both his arms broke nine-and-ninety castles
down,
Slew Vritra and smote Ahi dead.

3. This Indra is our gracious friend. He sends, like a full-streaming cow,
Riches in horses, kine, and corn.

V Surya

1. May the bright God drink glorious Soma-mingled meath, giving
the sacrifices lord unbroken life
He who, wind-urged, in person guards our offspring well, nourishes them
with food and shines o'er many a land.

2. Radiant, as high Truth, cherished, best at winning strength, Truth based
upon the statute that supports the heavens,
He rose, a light that kills Vritras and enemies, best slayer of the Dasyus,
Asuras, and foes.

3. This light, the best of lights, supreme, all conquering, winner of riches, is
exalted with high laud.
All-lighting, radiant, mighty as the Sun to see, he spreadeth wide unshaken
victory and strength.

VI Indra

1. O Indra, give us wisdom as a sire gives wisdom to his sons,
Guide us, O much-invoked, in this our way: may we still livc and look upon
the light!

2. Grant that no mighty foes, unknown, malevolent unhallowed, tread us to
the ground!
With thine assistance, hero, may we pass through all the waters that are
rushing down!

VII Indra

1. Protect us, Indra, each to-day, each to morrow, and each following day!
Through all the days shalt thou, Lord of the brave, preserve our singers
both by day and night!

2. A crushing warrior, passing rich, is Maghavan, endowed with all heroic strength.

Thine arms, O Satakratu, are exceeding strong, those arms,

which grasp the thunderbolt.

VIII Sarasvan

1. We call upon Sarasvan as unmarried men who long for wives,

As bounteous men who yearn for sons.

IX Sarasvati

1. Yea, she most dear amid dear streams-seven-sistered, loved with foundest love.

Sarasvati, hath earned our praise.

X Svitar. Brahmapaspati. Agni

1. May we attain that excellent glory of Savitar the God: So may he stimulate our prayers!

2. O Brahmanaspati, make thou Kakshivan Ausija a loud Chanter of flowing Soma juice!

3. Agni, thou pourest life: send down upon us food and vigorous strength; Drive thou misfortune far away!

XI Mitra-Varuva

1. So help ye us to riches, great celestial and terrestrial wealth

Vast is your sway among the Gods!

2. Carefully tending Law with law they have attained their vigorous might: Both Gods, devoid of guile, wax strong.

3. With rainy skies and streaming floods, Lords of the food that falls in dew,
A lofty seat have they attained.

XII Indra

I. They who stand round him as he moves harness the bright, the ruddy steed:
The lights shining in the sky.

2. On both sides to the car they yoke the two bay coursers dear to him,
Brown, bold, who bear the hero on.

3. Thou, making light where no light was, and form, O men where form was not,
Wast born together with the Dawns.

XIII Soma Pavamana

1. For thee this Soma is effused. O Indra: drink of this j uice; for thee the stream is flowing--
Soma, which thou thyself hast made and chosen, even Indu for thy special drink to cheer thee!

2. Like a capacious car hath it been harnessed, the mighty, to acquire abundant treasures.
Then in the sacrifice they shouted lauding all triumphs won by Nahus in the battle.

3. Flow onward like the potent band of Maruts, like that celestial host which none revileth!
Quickly be gracious unto us like waters, like sacrifice victorious, thousand-fashioned!

XIV Agni

1. O Agni, thou hast been ordained Hotar of every sacrifice, By Gods, among the race of men.
So with sweet-sounding tongues for us sacrifice nobly in this rite:
Bring thou the Gods and worship them

2. For, as disposer, Agni, God, most wise in sacrifices, thou Knowest straightway the roads and paths.

XV Agni

1. Immortal, Hotar-priest, and God, with wondrous power heleads the way,
Urging the congregations on.

2. Strong, he is set on deeds of strength. He is led forth in holy rites,
Sage who completes the sacrifice.

3. Excellent, he was made by thought. The germ of beings have gained.
Yea, and the Sire of active power.

XVI Agni

1. Pour on the juice the heated milk which hasteneth to heaven and. earth;
Bestow the liquid on the Bull!

2. These know their own abiding-place: like calves beside themother cows,
They come together with their kin.

3. Devouring in their greedy jaws, they make sustaining food irb heaven,
For Indra, Agni, homage, light.

XVII Indra

1. In all the worlds That was the best and highest whence sprang the mighty one, of splendid valour,
As soon as he is born he smites his foemen, he in whom all

who lend him aid are joyful foe

2. Grown mighty in his strength, of ample vigour, he as a strikes fear into the Dasa,
Eager to win the breathing and the breathless. All sang thy praise at banquet and oblation.

3. All concentrate on thee their mental vigour, what time these, once or twice, are thine assistants.
Blend what is sweeter than the sweet with sweetness: win quickly with our meath that meath in battle.

XVIII Indra

1. At the Trikadrukas the great and strong enjoyed the barley-brew. With Vishnu did he drink the pressed-out Soma juice, even as he would.
That hath so heightened him the great, the wide, to do his mighty work. So may the God attend the God, true Indu Indra who is true!

2. Brought forth together with wisdom and potent strength thou grewest great: with hero deeds subduing the malevolent, most swift in act;
Giving prosperity and lovely wealth to him who praiseth thee.
So may the God attend the God, true Indu Indra who is true!

3. So he resplendent in the battle overcame Krivi by might. He with his majesty bath filled the earth and heaven, and waxen strong.
One share of the libation bath he swallowed down: one share he left.
Enlighten us! So may the God attend the God, true Indu Indra who is true!

BOOK VII.

CHAPTER I.

I Indra

1. Praise, even as he is known, with song Indra the guardian of the kine,
The Son of Truth, Lord of the brave,

2. Hither have his bay steeds been sent, red steeds are on the sacred grass
Where we in concert sing our songs.

3. For Indra, thunder-armed, the kine have yielded mingled milk and meath,
What time he found them in the vault.

II Indra

1. Draw near unto our Indra who must be invoked in every fight!
Come, thou most mighty Vritra-slayer, meet for praise come to
libations and to hymns.

2. Thou art the best of all in sending bounteous gyifts, true art thou,, lordly
in thine act.
We claim alliance with the very glorious one, yea, with the
mighty Son of Strength.

III Soma Pavamana

I. They have drained forth from out the great depth of the sky the old
divine primeval milk that claims the laud:
They lifted up their voice to Indra at his birth.

2. Then, beautifully radiant, certain heavenly ones proclaimed their kinship with him as they looked thereon:
Savitar opens, as it were, the fold of heaven.

3. And now that thou, O Pavamana, art above this earth and heaven and all existence in thy might,
Thou shinest like a bull supreme among the herd.

IV Agni

1. O Agni, graciously announce this our good fortune to the Gods,
And this our newest hymn of praise!

2. Thou dealest gifts, resplendent one! nigh, as with wave of Sindhu, thou
Swift strearnest to the worshipper.

3. Give us a share of wealth most high, a share of wealth most near to us,
A share of wealth that is between.

V Indra

I from my Father have obtained deep knowledge of eternal Law;
I was born like unto the Sun.

2. After the ancient manner I, like Kanva, beautify my songs,
And Indra's self gains power thereby.

3. Whatever gishis have not praised thee, Indra, or have praised thee, wax
Mighty indeed when praised by me!

VI Agni

1. Agni, produced by strength, do thou with all thy fires accept our prayer:
With those that are with Gods, with those that are with men exalt our songs!

2. Forth come to us with all his fires that Agni, whose the mighty are,
Come, fully girt about with wealth for us and for our kith and kin!

3. Do thou, O Agni, with thy fires strengthen our prayer and sacrifices:
Incite them to bestow their wealth to aid our service of the Gods!

VII Soma Pavamana

1. Some, the men of old whose grass was trimmed addressed the hymn to
thee for mighty strength and for renown:
So, hero, urge us onward to heroic power'

2. All round about hast thou with glory pierced for us as 'twere a never-
failing well for men to drink,
Borne on thy way as 'twere in fragments from both arms.

3. Thou didst produce him, deathless one! for mortal man, for maintenance
of Law and lovely Amrita:
Thou evermore hast moved making wealth flow to us.

VIII Indra

1. Pour out the drops f or Indra; let him drink the meath of Soma Juice!
He through his majesty sends forth his bounteous gifts.

2. I spake to the bay coursers' Lord, to him who grants the boon. of wealth:
Now hear the son of Asva as he praises thee?

3. Never was any hero born before thee mightier than thou:
None certainly like thee in riches and in praise.

IX Indra

1. Thou wishest for thy kine a bull, lord of thy cows whom none may kill,

For those who long for his approach, for those who turn away from him.

X Agni

1. The God who giveth wealth accept the full libation poured to him!
Pour ye it out, then fill the vessel full again, for so the God regardeth you!

2. The Gods made him the Hotar-priest of sacrifice, oblationbearer, passing wise.
Agni gives wealth and valour to the worshipper, to man who offers up his gifts.

XI Agni

1. He hath appeared, best prosperer, in whom men lay their holy acts:
So may our songs of praise come nigh to Agni who was born to give the Arya strength.

2. Him before whom the people shrink when he performs his glorious deeds,
Him who wins thousands at the sacrifice, himself, that Agni, reverence with songs!

3. Agni of Divoddsa, God, comes forth like Indra in his might.
Rapidly hath he moved along his mother earth; he stands in high heaven's dwelling-place.

XII Agni

1. Agni, thou pourest life: send down upon us food and vigorous strength:
Drive thou misfortune far away!

2. Agni is Pavamana, Sage, Chief Priest of all the fivefold tribes; To him whose wealth is great we pray.

3. Skilled in thy task, O Agni, pour splendour with hero strength on us,
Granting me wealth that nourishes!

XIII Agni

1. O Agni, holy and divine with splendour and thy pleasant tongue. Bring
thou the Gods and worship them!

2. We pray thee bathed in butter, O bright-rayed! who lookest on the sun,
Bring the Gods hither to the feast!

3. Sage, we have kindled thee, the bright, the feaster on oblation, thee, O
Agni, great in sacrifice!

XIV Agni

I. Adorable in all our prayers, favour us, Agni, with thine aid.
What time the psalm is chanted forth!

2. Bring to us ever-conquering wealth, wealth, Agni, worthy of our choice,
Invincible in all our frays!

3. Grant us, O Agni, through thy grace wealth to support us evermore,
Thy favour so that we may live!

XV Agni

1. Let songs of ours speed Agni forth like a fleet courser in the race,
And we will win each prize through him

2. Agni! the host whereby we gain kine for ourselves with help from thee,-
That send us for the gain of wealth!

3. O Agni, bring us wealth secure, vast wealth in horses and in kine:
Oil thou the socket, turn the wheel!

4. O Agni, thou hast made the Sun, the eternal star, to mount the sky,
Giving the boon of light to men.

5. Thou, Agni, art the people's light, best, dearest, seated in thy shrine
Watch for the singer, give him life!

XVI Agni

1. Agni is head and height of heaven, the master of the earth is he:
He quickeneth the waters' seed.

2. Yea, Agni, thou as Lord of light rulest o'er choicest gifts may I,
Thy singer, find defence in thee

3. Upward, O Agni, rise thy flames, pure and resplendent, blazing high,
Thy lustres, fair effulgences.

CHAPTER II.

I Agni

1. Who, Agni, is thy kin, of men? who honours thee with sacrifice?
On whom dependent? who art thou?

2. The kinsman, Agni! of mankind, their well-beiaved friend art thou,
A friend whom friends may supplicate.

3. Bring Mitra, Varukia, bring the Gods hither to. our great sacrifice:
Bring them, O Agni, to thine home

II Agni

1. Meet to be worshipped and implored, showing in beauty through the gloom,
Agni, the strong, is kindled well.

2. Strong Agni is enkindled well, even as the horse that brings the Gods:
Men with oblations pray to him.

3. We will enkindle thee, the strong, we, hero! who axe strong ourselves,

III Agni

1. Thy mighty flames, O Agni, when thou art enkindled, rise on high,
Thy bright flames, thou refulgent one

2. Beloved! let my ladies full of sacred oil come nigh to thee.
Agni, accept our offerings!

3. I pray to Agni--may he hear!--the Hotar with sweet tones, the Priest,
Wondrously splendid, rich in light,

V Agni

1. O King, the potent and terrific envoy, kindled for strength, is
manifest in beauty.
He shines, observant, with his lofty splendour; chasing black night he
comes with white-rayed morning.

2. Having o'ercome the glimmering Black with beauty, and bringing forth
the Dame, the great Sire's daughter,
Holding aloft the radiant lights of Surya, as messenger of heaven he shines
with treasures.

3. Attendant on the blessed Dame the blessed hath come: the lover
followeth his sister.
Agni, far-spreading with conspicuous lustre, hath covered night with
whitely-shining garments.

VI Agni

1. What is the praise wherewith, O God, Angiras, Agni, Son of Strength,
We, after thine own wish and thought,

2. May serve thee, O thou Child of Power, and with what sacrifice's plan?
What reverent word shall I speak here?

VII Agni

1. Agni, come hither with thy fires; we choose thee as our Hotar; let
The proffered ladle filled with offerings balm thee, best of priests, to sit on
sacred grass!

2. For unto thee, O Angiras, O Son of Strength, move ladles in the sacrifice.

We pray to Agni, Child of Force, whose locks drop oil, foremost in sacrificial rites.

VIII Agni

1. Let our songs come anear to him beauteous and bright with piercing flame,
Our sacrifices with our homage unto him much-lauded, very rich, for help:

2. To Agni Jatavedas, to the Son of Strength, that he may give us precious gifts,

3. Immortal, from of old Priest among mortal men, whose tones are sweetest in the house!

X Agni

1. Invincible is Agni, he who goes before the tribes of men,
A chariot swift and ever new.

2. By bringing offerings unto him the mortal worshipper obtains
A home from him whose light is pure.

3. Inviolable power of Gods, subduing all his enemies, Agni is mightiest in fame.

XI Agni

1. May Agni, worshipped, bring us bliss: may the gift, blessed one! and sacrifice bring bliss,
Yea, may our eulogies bring bliss

2. Show forth the mind that brings success in war with fiends, wherewith thou conquerest in fight!

Bring down the many firm hopes of our enemies, and for thy victory let us win!

XII Agni

1. O Agni thou who art the Lord of wealth in kine, thou Son of Strength,
Bestow on us, O Jatavedas, high renown

2. He, Agni, kindled, good and wise, must be entreated with a. song;
Shine, thou of many forms, shine thou with wealth on us

3. And, Agni, shining of thyself by night and when the morning breaks,
Burn, thou whose teeth are sharp, against the Rakshasas

XIII Agni

1. Exerting all our strength with thoughts of power we glorify in speech,
Agni, your dear familiar friend, the darling guest of every house:

2. Whom, served with sacrificial oil, like Mitra, men presenting gifts,
Glorify with their songs of praise

3. Much-lauded Jatavedas, him who sends oblations up to heaven,
Prepared in service of the Gods.

XIV Agni

1. Agni, inflamed with fuel, in my song I sing, pure bright, and stedfast set in front at sacrifice.
Wise Jatavedas we implore with prayers for grace, the Sage, the Hotar-priest, bounteous, and void of guile.

2. Men, Agni, in each age, have made thee, deathless one, their envoy, offering-bearer, guard adorable.

With reverence Gods and mortals have established thee as everwatchful and almighty household Lord.

3. Though, Agni ordering the works and ways of both, as envoy of the Gods traversest both the realms.
When we lay claim to thy regard and gracious care, be thou to us a th rice-protecting friendly guard?

XV Agni

1. Still turning to their aim in thee the sacrificer's sister hymns
Have come to thee before the wind.

2. Even the waters find their place in him whose three fold sacred grass
Is spread unbound, unlimited.

3. The station of the bounteous God, by his unconquerable aid,
Hath a fair aspect like the Sun.

CHAPTER III.

I Indra

1. Men with their lauds are urging thee, Indra, to drink the Soma first.
The Ribhus in accord have lifted up their voice, and Rudras sung thee as the first.

2. Indra, at sacrifice, increased his manly strength, in the wild rapture of this juice:
And living men to-day, even as of old, sing forth their praises to his majesty.

II Indra-Agni

1. Indra and Agni! singers skilled in melody, with lauds, hymn you:
I choose you both to bring me food.

2. Indra and Agni! ye shook down, together, with one mightyr deed, The ninety forts which Dasas held.

3. To Indra and to Agni prayers go forward from the holy task, Along the path of sacred Law.

4. Indra and Agni, powers are yours, yours are oblations ano abodes: Good is your zealous energy.

III Indra

1. Indra, with all thy saving helps assist us, Lord of power and might!
For after thee we follow even as glorious bliss, thee, hero, finder-out of wealth!

2. Increaser of our steeds and multiplying kine, a golden well, G God, art thou,
For no one may impair the gift laid up in thee. Bring me whatever thing I ask!

IV Indra

1. For thou--come to the worshipper!--wilt find great wealth to make us rich.
Fill thyself full, O Maghavan, for gain of kine, full, Indra, forthe gain of steeds!

2. Thou as thy gift bestowest many hundred herds, yea, many thou-sands dost thou give.
With singers' hymns have we brought the fortrender near, singing to Indra for his grace.

V Agni

1. To him who dealeth out all wealth, the sweet-toned Hotar-priest of men,
To him, like the first vessels filled with savoury juice, to Agni let the lauds go forth!

2. Votaries, bounteous givers, deck him with their songs, even as the steed who draws the car.
To both, strong Lord of men! to kith and kin convey the bounties of our wealthy lords!

VI Varuna

1. Hear this my call, O Varuna, and show thy gracious love today:
Desiring help I long for thee!

VII Indra

1. O Hero, with what aid dost thou delight us, with what succour bring, Riches to those who worship thee?

VIII Indra

1. Indra, for service of the Gods, Indra while sacrifice proceeds, Indra, as worshippers, in battle-shock we call, Indra that we may win the spoil.

2. With might hath Indra spread out heaven and earth, with power hath indra lighten up the Sun. In Indra are all creatures closely held; in him meet the distilling Soma-drops.

IX Visvakarman

1. Bring, Visvakarman strengthened by oblation, thyself, thy body-'tis thine own-for worship
Let other men around us live in folly here let us have', a rich and liberal patron!

X Soma Pavamana

1. With this his golden splendour purifying him, he with his own allies subdues all enemies. as Sura with his own allies.
Cleansing himself with stream of juice he shines forth yellow-hued and red, when with his praisers he encompasses all forms, with praisers having seven mouths.

2. He moves intelligent directed to the east. The every beauteous car rivals the beams of light, the beautiful celestial car.
Hymns, lauding manly valour, came inciting Indra to success, that ye may be unconquered, both thy bolt and thou, both be unconquered in the war.

3. That treasure of the Panis thou discoveredst. Thou with the Mothers deckest thee in thine abode, with, songs of worship in thine home.

As 'twere from far away is heard the psalm where hymns resound in joy.
He, with the triple Dames red-hued, hath won life-power, he, gleaming,
hath won vital strength.

XI Pusan

1. Yea, cause our hymn to gain for us cattle and steeds and store of wealth,
That it may help us manfully!

XII Maruts

1. Heroes of real strength, ye mark either the sweat of him who toils,
Or his desire who supplicates.

XIII Visvedevas

1. The Sons of immortality shall listen to our songs of praise,
And be exceeding kind to us.

XIV Heaven and Earth

1. To both of you, O Heaven and Earth, we bring our lofty song of praise,
Pure pair! to glorify you both.

2. Ye sanctify each other's form by your own proper strength ye rule:
Further the sacrifice evermore!

3. Promoting and fulfilling, ye, mighty ones, perfect Mitra's law:
Ye sit around our sacrifice.

XV Indra

1. This is thine own. Thou drawest near, as turns a pigeon to his mate:
Thou carest, too, for this our prayer.

2. O hero, Lord of bounties, praised in hymns, may glorious fame and might
Be his who sings the laud to thee

3. Lord of a Hundred Powers, rise up to be our succour in this fight:
In other fights let us agree

XVI Oblations

1. Ye cows, protect the fount: the two mighty ones bless the sacrifice.
The handles twain are wrought of gold.

2. The pressing-stones are set at work: the meath is poured into the tank
At the out-shedding of the fount.

3. With reverence they drain the fount that circles with its wheel above.
Exhaustless, with the mouth below.

XVII Indra

1. Let us not tire or be afraid with thee, the mighty, for our friend!
May we see Turvasa and Yadu! thy great deed, O hero, must be glorified.

2. On his left hip the hero hath reclined himself: the proffered feast offends
him not.
The milk is blended with the honey of the bee: quickly come hither, haste,
and drink!

XVIII Indra

1. May these my songs of praise exalt thee, Lord, who hast abundant
wealth!
Men skilled in holy hymns, pure, with the hues of fire, have
sung them with their lauds to thee.

2. He, when a thousand Rishis have enhanced his might, hath like an ocean spread himself.

His majesty is praised as true at solemn rites, his power where holy singers rule.

XIX Indra

1. Good Lord of wealth is he to whom all Aryas, Dasas here belong.
Directly unto thee, the pious Rusama Paviru, is that wealth brought nigh.

2. In zealous haste the singers have sung forth a song distilling
fatness, rich in sweets.
Riches have spread among us and heroic strength, with us are flowing Soma-drops.

XX Soma Pavamana

1. Flow to us, Indu, very strong, effused, with wealth of kine and steeds,
And do thou lay above the milk thy radiant hue

2. Lord of the tawny, Indu, thou who art the Gods' most special food,
As friend to friend, for splendour be thou good to men!

3. Drive utterly, far away from us each godless, each voracious; foe;
O Indu, overcome and drive the false afar!

XXI Soma Pavamana.

1. They balm him, balm him over, balm him thoroughly, caress. the mighty strength and balm it with the meath.
They seize the flying Steer at the stream's breathing place cleansing with gold they grasp the animal herein.

2. Sing forth to Pavamana skilled in holy song! the juice is flowing onward like a mighty stream.

He glideth like a serpent from his ancient skin, and like a. playful horse the tawny Steer hath run.

3. Dweller in floods, King, foremost, he displays his might, set among living things as measure of days.

Distilling oil he flows, fair, billowy, golden-hued, borne on car of light, sharing on home with wealth.

BOOK VIII.

CHAPTER I.

I Agni

1. With all thy fires, O Agni, find pleasure in this our sacrifice,
And this our speech, O son of Strength!

2. Whate'er, in this perpetual course, we sacrifice to God and God,
That gift is offered but in thee.

3. May he be our beloved King and excellent sweet-toned Hotar may
We with bright fires be dear to him

II Indra

1. For you from every side we call Indra away from other men
Ours, and none others, may he be!

2. Unclose, our manly hero! thou for ever bounteous, yonder cloud
For us, thou irresistible

3. As the strong bull leads on the herds, he stirs the people with his might,
The ruler irresistible.

III Agni

1. Wonderful, with thy saving help, send us thy bounties, gracious Lord!
Thou art the charioteer, Agni, of earthly wealth: find rest and safety for our
seed!

2. Prosper our kith and kin with thy protecting powers inviolate, never
negligent!

Keep far from us, O Agni, all celestial wrath. and wickedness of godless men!

IV Vishnu

1. What, Vishnu, is the name that thou proclaimest when thou declaredst, I am Sipivishta?
Hide not this form from us, nor keep it secret, since thou didst wear another shape in battle.

2. This offering to-day, O Sipivishta, I, skilled in rules, extol, to thee the noble.
Yea, I, the poor and weak, praise thee, the mighty, who dwellest in the realm beyond this region.

3. O Vishnu, unto thee my lips cry Vashat! Let this mine offering, Sipivishta, please thee!
May these my songs of eulogy exalt thee! Do ye preserve us evermore with blessings!

V Vayu, Indra and Vayu

I. Vayu, the bright is offered thee, best of the meath, at morning rites.
Come thou to drink the Soma juice, God, longed for on thy team-drawn car!

2. O Vayu, thou and Indra are meet drinkers of these Soma draughts,
For unto you the drops proceed like waters gathering to the vale.

3. Vayu and Indra, mighty twain, borne on one chariot, Lords of strength,
Come to ouf succour with your steeds, that ye may drink the
Soma juice!

VI Soma Pavamana

1. Then thou, made beautiful by night, enterest into mighty deeds,
When prayers impel the golden-hued to hasten from Vivasvan's place.

2. We cleanse this gladdening drink of his, the juice which Indra chiefly drinks,
That which kine took into their mouths, oF old, and princes take it now.

3. Thy with the ancient psalm have sung to him as he is purified,
And sacred songs which bear the Dames of Gods have supplicated him.

VI Agni

1. With homage will I reverence thee, Agni, like a long-tailed steed,
Imperial Lord of holy rites.

2. May the far-striding Son of Strength, our friend who brings felicity,
Who pours his gifts like rain, be ours

3. From near and far away do thou, the everlasting, evermore
Protect us from the sinful man!

VIII Indra

1. Thou in thy battles, Indra, art subduer of all hostile bands.
Father art thou, all-conquering, cancelling the curse, thou victor of the vanquisher!

2. The earth and heaven cling close to thy victorious might, as sire and mother to their child.
When thou attackest Vritra, all the hostile bands shrink and faint, Indra, at thy wrath.

IX Indra

1. The sacrifice made Indra great when he unrolled the earth, and made

Himself a diadem in heaven.

2. In Soma's ecstasy Indra spread the firmament and realms of light,
When he cleft Vala limb from limb.

3. Showing the hidden, he drave forth the cows for the Angirasas,
And Vala he cast headlong down.

X Indra

1. Thou speedest down to succour us this-ever-conquering God of yours,
Him who is drawn to all our songs;

2, The warrior whom none may wound, the Soma-drinker ne'er o'erthrown,
The chieftain of resistless might.

3. O Indra, send us riches, thou omniscient, worthy of our hymns:
Help us in the decisive fray!

XI Indra

1. That lofty power and might of thine, thy strength and thine intelligence,
And thy surpassing thunderbolt, the wish makes keen.

2. O Indra, heaven and earth augment thy manly force and thy renown:
The waters and the mountains stir and urge thee on:

3. Vishnu in the lofty ruling power, Varuna, Mitra sing thy praise:
In thee the Maruts' company have great delight.

XII Agni

1. O Agni, God, the people sing reverent praise to thee for strength:
With terrors trouble thou the foe

2. Wilt thou not, Agni, lend us aid to win the cattle, win the wealth?
Maker of room, make room for us

3. In the great fight cast us not off, Agni, as one who bears a load:
Snatch up the wealth and win it all!

XIII Indra

1. Before his hot displeasure all the peoples, all the men bow down,
As rivers bow them to the sea.

2. Even fiercely-moving Vritra's head he served with his thunderbolt,
His mighty hundred-knotted bolt.

3. That might of his shone brightly forth when Indra brought together, like
A skin, the worlds of heaven and earth.

XIV Indra

1. Kind-thoughted is the noble, gladdening, friendly one.

2. Approach, O beauteous hero, this auspicious pair that draws the car!
These two are coming near to us.

3. Bend lowly down, as 'twere, your beads: be stands amid the water-flood,
Pointing with his ten horns the way.

CHAPTER II.

I Indra

1. Pressers, blend Soma juice for him, each draugbt most excellent, for him
The brave, the: hero, for his joy!

2. The two stroing bay steeds, voked by prayer, hither shall bring to us our
friend,
Indra, song-lover, through our songs.

3. The Vritra-slayer drinks the juice. May he who gives a hundred
aids
Approach, nor stay afar from usl

II Indra

1. Let the drops pass within thee as the rivers flow into the sea
O Indra, naught excelleth thee.

2. 'Thou' wakeful hero, by thy might hast taken food of Soma juice,
Which, Indra, is within thee now.

3. O Indra, Vritra-slayer, let Soma be ready for thy maw, The drops be
ready for thy forms!

III Agni

1. Help, thou who knowest lauds, this work, a lovely hymn in Rudra's
praise,
Adorable in every house

2. May this our God, great, limitless, smoke-bannered, excellently bright,
Urge us to holy thought and wealth

3. Like soma rich lord of men, may he, Agni, the banner of the Gods,
Refulgent, hear us through our lauds!

IV Indra

1. Sing this, beside the flowing juice, to him, your hero, much invoked,
To please him as a mighty Bull!

2. He, excellent, withholdeth not his bounteous gift of wealth in kine.
When lie bath listened to our songs.

3. May he with might unclose for us the cow's stall, whosesoe'er it be,
To which the Dasyu-slayer goes!

V Vishnu

1. Through all this world strode Vishnu: thrice his foot he planted, and the whole
Was gathered in his footstep's dust.

2. Vishnu, the guardian, he whom none deceiveth, made three steps, thenceforth
Establishing his high decrees.

3. Look ye on Vishnu's works whereby the friend of Indra, close allied,
Hath let his holy ways be seen

4. The princes evermore behold that loftiest place of Vishnu, like
An eye extended through the heavens.

5. This, Vishou's station most sublime, the sages, ever-vigilant,
Lovers of holy song, light up.

6. May the Gods help and favour us out of the place whence Vishnu strode
Over the back and ridge of earth.

VI Indra

1. Let none, no, not thy worshippers, delay thee far away from us!
Even from far away come thou unto our feast, or listen it already here!

2. For here, like rites on honey, those who pray to thee sit by the juice that
they have poured.
Wealth-craving singers have on Indra set their hope, as men set foot upon
a car.

VII Indra

1. Sung is the song of ancient time: to Indra have ye said the prayer.
They have sung many a Brihati of sacrifice, poured forth the worshipper's
many thoughts.

2. Indra hath tossed together mighty stores of wealth, and both the worlds,
yea, and the sun.
Pure, brightly-shining, mingled with the milk, the draughts of Soma have
made Indra glad.

VIII Soma Pavamana

1. For Vritra-slaying Indra, thou, Soma, art poured that he may drink,
And for the guerdon-giving man, the hero sitting in his seat.

2. Friends, may the princes, ye and we, obtain this most resplendent one,
Gain him who hath the smell of strength, win him whose home is very
strength!

3. Him with the fleece they purify, brown, golden-hued, beloved of all.

Who with exhilarating juice flows forth to all the deities.

IX Indra

1. Indra whose wealth is in thyself, what mortal will attack this man?
The strong will win the spoil on the decisive day through faith in thee, O
Maghavan!

2. In battles with the foe urge on our mighty ones who give the treasures
dear to thee
And may we with our princes, Lord of tawny steeds! pass through all peril,
led by thee!

X Indra

1. Come, priest, and of the savoury juice pour forth a yet more gladdening
draught!
So is the hero praised who ever prospers us.

2. Indra, whom tawny coursers bear, praise such as thine, preeminent,
None by his power or by his goodness hath attained.

3. We, seeking glory, have invoked this God of yours, the Lord of wealth,
Who must be magnified by constant sacrifice.

XI Agni

1. Sing praise to him, the Lord of light. The Gods have made the God to be
their messenger,
To bear oblation to the Gods.

2. Agni, the bounteous giver, bright with varied flames, laud thou, O singer
Sobhari,
Him who controls this sacred food with Soma blent, who hath first claim to
sacrifice!

XII Soma Pavamana

1. Expressed by stones, O Soma, and urged through the long wool of the sheep,
Thou, entering the press-boards, even as men a fort, goldbued, hast settled in the vats.

2. He beautifies himself through the sheep's long fine wool, the bounteous, like the racing steed,
Even Soma Pavamana who shall be the joy of sages and of holy bards.

XIII Indra

1. Here, verily, yesterday we let the Thunder-wielder drink his fill.
Bring him the juice poured forth in sacrifice to-day! Now range you by the glorious one!

2. Even the wolf, the savage beast that rends the sheep, follows the path of his decrees.
So graciously accepting, Indra, this our praise, with wondrous thought come forth to us!

XIV Indra-Agni

1. Indra and Agni, in your deeds of might ye deck heaven's lucid realms:
Famed is that hero strength of yours.

2. To Indra and to Agni prayers go forward from the holy task.
Along the path of sacred Law.

3. Indra and Agni, powers are yours, yours are oblations and abodes:
Good is your zealous energy.

XV Indra

1. Who knows what vital power he wins, drinking beside the flowing juice? This is the fair-cheeked God who, joying in the draught, breaks down the castles in his strength.

2. As a wild elephant rushes on, this way and that way mad with
heat,
None may restrain thee, yet come hither to the draught! Thou, movest mighty in thy power.

3. When he, the terrible, ne'er o'erthrown, stedfast, made ready for the fight--
When Indra Maghavan lists to his praiser's call, he will not stand aloof, but come.

XVI Soma Pavamana

1. The Pavamanas have been poured, the brilliant drops of Soma juice,
For holy lore of every kind.

2. From heaven, from out the firmament hath PavamAna been effused
Upon the back and ridge of earth.

3. The Pavamanas have been shed, the beautified swift Somadrops,
Driving all enemies afar.

XVII Indra-Agni

I. Indra and Agni I invoke, joint-victors, bounteous, unsubdued,
Foe-slayers, best to win the spoil.

2. Indra and Agni, singers skilled in melody hymn you bringing lauds:
I choose you both to bring me food.

3. Together, with one mighty deed, Indra and Agni, ye shook down.

The ninety forts which Dasas held.

XVIII Agni

1. O Child of Strength, to thee whose look is lovely, with oblations we,
O Agni, have poured forth our songs.

2. To thee for shelter are we come, as to the shade from fervent heat,
Agni, who glitterest like gold

3. Mighty as one who slays with shafts, or like a bull with sharpened horn,
Agni, thou brakest down the forts.

XIX Agni

1. To give eternal glow, we pray Vaisvanara the holy one, Lord of the light
of sacrifice.

2. Who, furthering the light of Law, hath spread himself to meet this work:
He sends the seasons, mighty one.

3. Love of what is and what shall be, Agni, in his beloved forms,
Shines forth alone as sovran Lord.

CHAPTER III.

I Agni

1. Wise Agni, in the ancient way, making his body beautiful,
Hath been exalted by the sage.

2. I invoke the Child of Strength, Agni whose glow is bright and pure,
In this well-ordered sacrifice.

3. So, Agni, rich in many friends, with fiery splendour seat thyself.
With Gods upon our sacred grass!

II Soma Pavamana

1. O thou with stones for arms, thy powers, rending the fiends, have raised
themselves:
Drive off the foes who compass us

2. Hence conquering with might when car meets car, and when the prize is
staked,
With fearless heart will I sing praise.

3. None, evil-minded, may assail this Pavamana's holy laws
Crush him who fain would fight with thee!

4. For Indra to the streams they urge the tawny rapture-dropping steed,
Indu, the bringer of delight.

III Indra

1. Come hither, Indra, with bay steeds, joyous, with tails like peacocks' plumes!
Let no men check thy course as fowlers stay the bird: pass o'er them as o'er desert lands!

2. Vritra's devourer, he who burst the cloud, brake forts, and drave the floods,
Indra, who mounts his chariot at his bay steeds' cry, shatters e'en things that stand most firm.

3. Like pools of water deep and full, like kine thou cherishest thy might;
Like the milch-cows that go well-guarded to the mead, like water-brooks that reach the lake.

IV Indra

1. Even as the wild bull, when he thirsts, goes to the desert's watery pool,
Come hither quickly both at morning and at eve, and with the Kanvas drink thy fill!

2. May the drops gladden thee, Lord Indra, and obtain bounty for him who pours the juice!
Soma, shed in the press, thou stolest and didst drink, and hence hast won surpassing might.

V Indra

I. Thou as a God. O mightiest, verily blessest mortal man.
O Maghavan, there is no comforter but thou: Indra, I speak my words to thee.

2. Let not thy bounteous gifts, let not thy saving help all fail us good Lord, at any time!
And measure out to us, thou lover of man-kind, all riches hitherward from men

VI Dawn

I. This Lady, excellent and kind, after her sister shining forth, Daughter of Heaven, hath shown herself.

2. Red, like a mare, and beautiful, holy, the mother of the kine, The Dawn became the Asvins' friend.

3. Yea, and thou art the Asvins', friend the mother of the cows art thou: O Dawn, thou rules over wealth

VII Asvins

1. Now Morning with her earliest light shines forth, dear daughter of the Sky:
High, Asvins, I extol your praise

2. Children of Ocean, mighty ones, discoverers of riches, Gods,
Finders of treasure through our prayer!

3. Your lofty coursers hasten over the everlasting realm, whea your car flies with winged steeds.

VIII Dawn

1. O Dawn who hast a store of wealth, bring unto us that splendid gift
Wherewith we may support children and children's sons

2. Thou radiant Lady of sweet strains, with wealth of horses and of kine
Shine thou on us this day, O Dawn, auspiciously

3. O Dawn who hast a store of wealth, yoke red steeds to thy car to-day.
Then bring us all delight and all felicities

IX Asvins

1. O Asvins, wonderful in act, do ye unanimous direct
Your chariot to our home wealthy in kine and gold!

2. Hither may they who wake at dawn bring, to drink Soma, both the Gods,
Health-givers, wonder-workers, borne on paths of gold!

3. Ye who brought down the hymn from heaven, a light that giveth light to men,
Do ye, O Asvins, bring strength hither unto us!

X Agni

I think of Agni who is kind, whom, as their home, the milch-kine seek;
Whom fleet-foot coursers seek as home, and strong enduring, steeds as home.
Bring food to those who sing thy praise!

2. For Agni, God of all mankind, gives the strong courser to theman.
Agni gives ready gear for wealth, he gives the best when he ix pleased.
Bring food to those who sing thy praise!

3. The Agni who is praised as kind, to whom the milch-kine come. in herds,
To whom the racers, swift of foot, to whom our wellborn princes come.
Bring food to those who sing thy praise!

XI Dawn

1. O heavenly Dawn, awaken us to ample opulence today,
Even as thou didst waken us with Satyasravas, Vayya's, Son, high-born!
delightful with thy steeds!

2. Daughter of heaven, thou dawnedst of Sunitha, Suchadratha's son;

So dawn thou on one mightier still, on Satyasravas, Vayya's son, high-born! delightful with thy steeds!

3. So bringing treasure, shine to-day on us, thou daughter, of the Sky,
As on one mightier thou hast dawned, on Satyasravas, Vayya's son, high-born! delightful with thy steeds!

XII Asvins

1. To meet your treasure-bringing car, the car that is most dear to us,
Asvins the Rishi is prepared, your worshipper with, songs of praise. Lovers of sweetness, hear my call

2. Pass, Asvins, over all away. May I obtain you for myself,
Wonderful, with your golden paths, most gracious, bringers of the flood!
Lovers of sweetness, hear my call!

3. Come to us, O ye Asvins twain, bringing your precious treasures, come
Ye Rudras, on your paths of gold, rejoicing, with your store of wealth!
Lovers of sweetness, hear my call!

XIII Agni

1. Agni is wakened by the people's fuel to meet the Dawn who cometh like a milch-cow.
Like young trees shooting up on high their branches, his flames mounting to the vault of heaven.

2. For the Gods' worship hath the priest been wakened: kind Agni hath arisen erect at morning.
Kindled, his radiant might is made apparent, and the great God hath been set free from darkness.

3. When he hath roused the line of his attendants, with the bright milk bright Agni is anointed.

Then is prepared the effectual oblation, which spread in front, with tongues, erect, he drinketh,

XIV Dawn

1. This light is come, amid all lights the fairest: born is the brilliant, far-extending brightness.
Night, sent away for Savitar's uprising, hath yielded up a birthplace for the morning.

2. The fair, the bright is come with her white offspring to her the Dark one hath resigned her dwelling.
Akin, immortal, following each other, changing their colours both the heavens move onward.

3. Common, unending is the sisters' pathway: taught by the Gods alternately they travel,
Fair-formed, of different hues and yet one-minded, Night and Dawn clash not, neither do they tarry.

XV Asvins

1. Agni, the bright face of the Dawns, is shining: the singers' pious voices have ascended.
Borne on your chariot, Asvins, turn you hither, and come unto our brimming warm libation!

2. Most frequent guests, they scorn not what is ready: even now the lauded Asvins are beside us.
With promptest aid they come at morn and evening, the worshipper's most healthful guards from trouble.

3. Yea, come at milking-time, at early morning, at noon of day, and when the Sun is setting,

By day, at night, with most auspicious favour! Not only now the draught hath drawn the Asvins.

XVI Dawn

1. These Dawns have raised their banner: in the eastern half of middle air they spread abroad their shining light.
Like heroes who prepare their weapons for the fray, the cows are coming on, the mothers, red of hue.

2. Rapidly have the ruddy beams of light shot up: the red cows have they harnessed, easy to be yoked.
The Dawns have made their pathways as in former times: redhued, they have attained refulgent brilliancy.

3. They sing their song like women active in their tasks, along their common path hither from far away,
Bringing refreshment to the liberal devotee, yea, all things to the worshipper who pours the juice.

XVII Asvins

1. Agni is wakened: Surya riseth from the earth. Bright Dawn hath opened out the mighty twain with light.
The Asvins have equipped their chariot for the course. God Savitar hath roused the world in sundry ways.

2. When, O ye Asvins, ye equip your mighty car, with fatness and with honey balm, ye twain, our power!
To our devotion give victorious strength in war: may we win riches in the heroes' strife for spoil!

3. Nigh to us come the Asvins' lauded three wheeled car, the car laden with meath and drawn by fleet-foot steeds,

Three-seated, opulent, bestowing all delight: may it bring weal to us, to cattle and to men!

XVIII Soma Pavamana

1. Thy streams that never fail or waste flow forth like showers of rain from heaven,
To bring a thousand stores of wealth.

2. He, flows beholding on his way all well-beloved sacred lore,
Green-tinted, brandishing his arms.

3. He, when the people deck him like a docile king of elephants,
Sits as a falcon in the wood.

4. So bring thou hitherward to us, Indu, while thou art purified.
All treasures both of heaven and earth!

BOOK IX.

CHAPTER I.

I Soma Pavamana

1. Forward have flowed the streams of power, of this the mighty one effused,
Of him who waits upon the Gods.

2. The singers praise him with their song, and learned priests adorn the steed
Born as thelight that merits laud.

3. These things thou winnest quickly, while men cleanse thee, Soma, nobly rich!

II Indra

1. This Brahman, comer at the due time, named Indra, is renowned and praised.

2. To thee alone, O Lord of Strength, go, as it were, all songs of praise.

3. Like streams of water on their way, let bounties, Indra, flow from thee!

III Indra

1. Even as a car to give us aid, we draw thee nigh to favour us,
Strong in thy deeds, quelling attack, Indra, Lord, mightiest! of the brave.

2. Great in thou power and wisdom, strong, with thought that comprehendeth all!
Wide hast thou spread in majesty.

3. Thou very mighty one, whose hands by virtue of thy greatness wield
The golden bolt that beaks its way!

IV Agni

1. He who hath lighted up the joyous castle, wise courser like the steed of cloudy heaven,
Bright like the Sun with hundredfold existence

2. He, doubly born, hath spread in his effulgence through the three luminous realms, through all the regions,
Best sacrificing Priest where waters gather.

3. Priest doubly born, he through his love of glory hath in his keeping all things worth the choosing.
The man who brings him gifts hath noble offspring.

V Agni

1. Agni, with hymns may we now accomplish that which thou lovest,
Strength, like a horse auspicious, with service!

2. For, Agni, thou art now the promoter of strength auspicious,
Lofty sacrifice, power effective.

3. Through these our praises, come thou to meet us, bright as the sunlight,
Agni, kindly with all thy faces!

VI Agni

1. Immortal Jatavedas, thou bright-hued refulgent gift of Dawn.
Agni, this day to him who pays oblations bring the Gods who waken with the morn!

2. For thou art offering-bearer, well-loved messenger, and charioteer of holy rites.

Accordant with the Asvins and with Dawn grant us heroic strength and lofty fame!

VII Indra

1. The old hath waked the young Moon from his slumber who runs his circling course with many round him

Behold the God's high wlsdom in its greatness: he who died yesterday to-day is living.

2. Strong is the red Bird In his strength, great hero, who from of old bath had no nest to dwell in.

That which he knows is truth and never idle: he wins and gives the wealth desired of many.

3. Through these Thunderer gained strong manly vigour, through whom he waxed in stren gth to slaughter Vritra;

These who through might of actual operation sprang forth as Gods in course of Law and Order.

VIII Maruts

1. Here is the Soma ready pressed: of this the Maruts, yea, of this Self-luminous, the Asvins, drink.

2. Of this, moreover, purified, set in three places, procreant, Drink Varuna, Mitra, Aryaman.

3. Yea, Indra, like the Hotar-priest, will in the early morning drink,

At pleasure, of the milky juice:

IX Surya

1. Verily, Surya, thou art great; truly, Aditya, thou art great.
O most admired for greatness of thy majesty, God, by thy greatn.ess thou art great.

2. Yea, Surya, thou art great in fame: thou evermore, O God, art great.
Thou by thy greatness art the Gods' High-Priest, divine, farspread unconquerable light.

X Indra

1. Come, Lord of rapturous joys, to our libations with thy bay steeds, come
With bay steeds to our flowing juice!

2. Known as best Vritra-slayer erst, as Indra $atakratu, come
With bay steeds to our flowing juice!

3. For, Vritra-slayer, thou art he who drinks these drops of Soma come
With bay steeds to our flowing juice!

XI Indra

1. Bring to the wise, the great, who waxeth mighty your offerings and make ready your devotion.
Go forth to many tribes as man's controller!

2. For Indra the sublime, the far-pervading, have singers generateo prayer and praises;
The sages never violate his statutes.

3. The choirs have established Indra King for ever for victory him, whose anger is resistless:
And for the bays' Lord strengthened those he loveth.

XII Indra

1. If I, O Indra, were the lord of riches ample as thine own,
I would support the singer, God who scatterest wealth! and, not abandon him to woe.

2. Each day would I enrich the man who sang my praise, in whatsoever place he were.
No kinship is there better, Maghavan, than thine: a father even, is no more.

XIII Indra

1. Here thou the call of the juice-drinking press-stone: mark thou the sage's hymn who sings and lauds thee!
Take to thine inmost self these adorations!

2. I know and ne'er forget the hymns and praises of thee, theconqueror, of thy power immortal.
Thy name I ever utter, self-refulgent!

3. Among mankind many are thy libations, and many a time the pious sage invokes thee.
O Maghavan, be not long distant from us!

XIV Indra

1. Sing strength to Indra that shall. set his chariot in the foremost place!
Giver of room in closest fight, slayer of foes in shock of war, be thou our great encorager! Let the weak bowstrings break upon the bows of our weak mies!

2. Thou didst destroy the Dragon: thou sentest the rivers down to Earth.
Foeless, O Indra, wast thou born. Thou tendest well each choicest thing. Therefore we draw us close to thee. Let the weak bowstrings break upon the bows of our weak enemies!

Destroyed be all malignitics and all our enemy's designs!

3. Thy bolt thou castest at the foe, O Indra, who would smite us dead: thy liberal bounty gives us wealth. Let the weak bowstrings break upon the bows of our weak enemies!

XV Indra

1. Rich be the praiser of one rich and liberal, Lord of days! like thee:
High rank be his who lauds the juice!

2. His wealth who hath no store of kine hath ne'er found out recited laud,
Nor song of praises that is sung.

3. Give us not, Indra, as a prey unto the scornful or the proud:
Help, mighty one, with power and might!

XVI Indra

1. Come hither, Indra, with thy bays, come thou to Kanva's eulogy!
Ye by command of yonder Dyaus, God bright by day! have gone to heaven.

2. The stones' rim shakes the Soma here like a wolf worrying a sheep.
Ye by command of yonder Dyaus, God bright by day I have gone to heaven.

3. May the stone bring thee as it speaks, the Soma-stone with ringing voice!
Ye by command of yonder Dyaus, God bright by day! have gone to heaven.

XVII Soma Pavamana

1. For Indra flow most rich in sweets, O Soma, bringing him delight!

2. Bright, meditating sacred song, these juices have sent Vayu forth.

3. They were sent forth to feast the Gods, like chariots speeding in the race.

XVIII Agni

1. Agni I deem our Hotar priest, munificent wealth-giver, Son of Strength, who knoweth all that is even as the Sage who knoweth all.
Lord of fair rites, a God with form erected turning to the Gods, he when the flame hath sprung forth from the holy oil, the offered fatness, longs for it as it grows bright.

2. We, sacrificing, call on the best worshipper thee eldest of Angirasas, singer! with hyrnns, thee, brilliant one! with singers' hymn;
Thee, wandering round, as 'twere the sky, thee who art Hotar-priest of men, whom, Bull with hair of flame, the people must observe, tile people that he speed them on.

3. He with his blazing Power refulgent far and wide, he verily it iswho conquers demon foes, conquers the demons like an axe:
At whose close touch things solid partg and what is stable yields he keeps his ground and flinches not,like trees. Subduing all from the skilled archer flinches not.

CHAPTER II.

I Agni

1. O Agni, strength and fame are thine: thy fires blaze forth on high, O thou refulgent God!
Sage, passing bright, thou givest to the worshipper with power, the wealth that merits laud.

2. With brilliantg purifying sheen, with perfect sheen thou liftest up thyself in light.
Thou, visiting both thy mothers, aidest them as son; thou joinest close the earth and heaven.

3. O Jatavedas, Son of Strength, rejoice thyself, gracious, in our fair hymns and songs!
In thee have they heaped viands various, many formed; wealthborn, of wondrous help are they.

4. Agni, spread forth, as ruler, over living things: give wealth, to
us, immortal God!
Thou shinest out from beauty fair to look upon: thou leadest
us to beauteous Power.

5. I laud the Sage, who orders sacrifice, who hath great riches under his control.
Thou givest blest award of good, and plenteous food, thou givest wealth that wins success.

6. The men have set before them, for his favour, Agni, strong, visible to all, the holy.

Thee, Lord divine, with ears to hear, most famous, mens' generations magnify with praise-songs.

II Agni

1. Agni, he conquers by thine aid that brings him store of valiant sons and does great deeds,
Whose bond of friendship is thy choice.

2. Thy spark is black and crackling; kindled in due time, O bounteous, it is taken up.
Thou art the dear friend of the mighty Mornings: thou shinest in glimmerings of the night.

III Agni

1. Him, duly coming, as their germ have plants received: this Agni have maternal Waters brought to life.
So, in like manner, do the forest trees and plants bear him within them and produce him evermore.

IV Agni

1. Agni grows bright for Indra: he shines far resplendent in the sky:
He sends forth offspring like a queen.

V Agni

1. The sacred hymns love him who wakes and watches: to him who watches the holy verses.
This Soma saith to him Who wake my dwelling in thy friendship.

VI Agni

1. Agni is watchful, and the Richas love him: Agni is watchful, Sama hymns approach him.
Agni is watchful, to him saith this Soma, I rest and have my dwelling in thy friendship.

VII Gods

1. Praise to the friends who sit in front! to those seated together,praise
I use the hundred-footed speech speech.

2. I use the hundred-footed speech, I sing what hath a thousand paths,
Gayatra, Trishtup, Jagat hymn.

3. Gayatra, Trishtup, Jagat hymn,the forms united and complete,
Have the Gods made familiar friends.

VIII Agni

1. Agni, is light, light is Agni, Indra is light, light is Indra
Surya is light, light is Surya.

2. O Agni, turn again with strength, turn thou again with food and life:
Save us again from grief and woe!

3. O Agni, turn again with wealth sprinkle thou us from everyside.
With thine own all-supporting stream!

IX Indra

1. If I, O Indra, were like thee, the single ruler over wealth.
My worshipper should be rich in kine.

2. I should be fain, O Lord of power, to strengthen and enrich thesage,
Where I the ford of herds of kine.

3. Thy goodness, Indra, is a cow yielding in plenty kine and steeds.
To worshippers who press the juice.

X The Waters

1. Yea, Waters, ye bring health and bliss: so help ye us to energy.
That we may look on great delight!

2. Give us a portion of the dew, the most auspicious that ye have,
Like mothers in their longing love!

3. For you we gladly go to hirn to whose abode ye speed us on,
And, Waters, give us procreant strength!

XI Vata

1. May Vata breathe his balm on us, healthful, delightful to our heart:
May he prolong our days of life!

2. Thou art our father, Vata, yea, thou art our brother and our friend:
So give us strength that we may live!

3. The store of Amrit that laid away yonder, O Vata, in thine home--
Give us strength that we may live!

XII Agni

1. The fleet steed wearing divers forms, the eagle bearing his golden raiment to his birthplace,
Clothed in due season with the light of Surya, red, hath begot the sacrifice in person.

2. Multiform seed he laid in waters, lustre which gathered on the earth and there developed.

In the mid-air establishing his greatness, he cries aloud, seed of the vigorous courser.

3. He hath, enduing thousand robes that suit him, as sacrifice upheld the light of Surya,
Giver of ample gifts in hundreds, thousands, supporter of the heavens, earth's Lord and ruler.

XIII Vena

1. They gaze on thee with longing in their spirit, as on a strong-winged bird that mounteth sky-ward;
On thee with wings of gold, Varuna's envoy, the Bird that hasteneth to the home of Yama.

2. Erect, to heaven hath the Gandharva mounted, pointing at us his many-coloured weapons:
Clad in sweet raiment beautiful to look on, for he, as light, produceth forms that please us..

3. When as a spark he cometh ilear the ocean, looking with vulture's eye as Law commandeth,
His lustre, joying in its own bright splendour, maketh dear glories in the loftiest region.

CHAPTER III.

I Indra

1. Swift, rapidly striking, like a bull who sharpens his horns, terrific, stirring up the people.
With eyes that close not, bellowing, sole hero, Indra subdued at once a hundred armies.

2. With him loud-roaring, ever watchful victor, bold, hard to overthrow, rouser of battle,
Indra. the strong, whose hand bears arrows, conquer, ye heroes, now, now vanquish in the combat!

3. He rules with those who carry shafts and quivers, Indra who with his band brings hosts together,
Foe-conquering strong of arm the Soma-drinker, with mighty bow, shooting with well-laid arrows.

II Brihaspati. Indra

1. Brihaspati, fly with thy chariot hither, slayer of demons, driving off our foemen!
Be thou protector of our cars, destroyer, victor in battle, breaker-up of armies!

2, Conspicuous. by thy strength, firm, foremost fighter, mighty and fierce, victorious, all-subduing,
The Son of Conquest, passing men and heroes, kinewinner, mount thy conquering car, O Indra!

3. Cleaver of stalls, kine-winner, armed with thunder, who quells an army and with might destroys it--
Follow him, brothers! quit yourselves like heroes, and like this Indra show your zeal and courage!

III Indra. Brihaspati

1. Piercing with conquering strength the cow-stalls, Indra, pitiless hero with unbounded anger,
Victor in fight, unshaken and resistless--may he protect our armies in our battles!

2. Indra guide these! Brihaspati, and Soma, the guerdon and the sacrifice precede them;
And let the banded Maruts march in forefront of heavenly hosts that conquer and demolish!

3. Ours be the potent host of mighty Indra, King Varuna the Maruts, and Adityas!
Uplifted is the shout of Gods who conquer, hightninded Gods who cause the worlds to tremble.

IV Indra.Maruts

1. Bristle thou up, O Maghavan, our weapons: excite the spirits, of my warring heroes!
Urge on the strong steed's might, O Vyitra-slayer, and let the din of conquering cars go upward

2. May Indra aid us when our flags are gathered: victorious be ther arrows of our army!
May our brave men of war prevail in battle. Ye Gods, protect us in the shout of onset!

That army of the foemen, O ye Maruts, which, striving in its. mighty strength, approaches,
Hide ye and bury it in pathless darkness that not a man oF them may know the other!

V Agha

1. Bewildering the senses of our foemen, seize thou their bodies, and depart, O Agha!
Attack them, set their hearts on fare with sorrows; so let our foes abide in utter darkness!

2. Advance, O heroes, win the day, May Indra be your sure defence!
Mighty and awful be your arms, that none may wound or injure you!

3. Loosed from the bowstring fly away, thou arrows sharpened by our prayer!
Go to the foemen, strike them home, and let not one be left alive!

VI Indra and others

1. Let ravens and strong-pinioned birds pursue them: yea, let that army be the food of vultures!
Indra, let none escape, no sin-remover: behind them all let following birds be gathered!

2. This host of foemen Maghavan! that cometh on in warlike show--
Meet it, O Vritra-slayer, thou, Indra, and Agni, with your flames!

3. There where the flights of arrows fall like boys whose locks are yet unshorn.
Even there may Brahmanaspati, may Aditi protect us well, protect us well through all our days!

VII Indra

1. Drive Rakshasas and foes away, break thou in pieces Vritra's jaws:
O Vritra-slaying Indra, quell the foeman's wrath who threatens us!
O Indra, beat our foes away, humble the men who challenge us:
Send down to nether darkness him who seeks to do us injury!

2. Strong, ever-youthful are the arms of Indra, fair unassailable, never to be vanquished:
These first let him employ when need hath come on us, wherewith the Asuras' great might was overthrown.

VIII Soma, Varuna

1. Thy vital parts I cover with thine armour: with immortality King Soma clothe thee!
Varuna give thee what is more than ample, and in thy victory may Gods be joyful!

2. Blind, O my foemen, shall ye be, even as headless serpents are
May Indra slay each best of you when Agni's flame hath struck you down!

3. Whoso would kill us, whether he be a stranger foe or one of us,
May all the Gods discomfit him! My nearest, closest mail is prayer, my closest armour and defence.

IX Indra. All-Gods

1. Like a dread wild beast roaming on the mountain thou hast approached us from the farthest distance.
Whetting thy bolt and thy sharp blade, O Indra, crush thou the foe and scatter those who hate us!

2. Gods, may our ears hear that which is auspicious, may our eyes see that which is good, ye holy!

Extolling you with still strong limbs and bodies, may we attain the age by Gods appointed!

3. Illustrious far and wide, may Indra bless us, may Pushan bless us, master of all riches!
May Tarkshya with uninjured fellies bless us! Brihaspati bestow on us his favour! Brihaspati bestow on us his favour!

Read these similar books for free at forgottenbooks.org:

Clarence Darrow on Religion

Mark Twain on Religion

The Rig Veda

The Yajur Veda

The Texts of the White Yajurveda

The Hymns of the Atharvaveda, Vol. 1 of 2

The Atharvaveda

A Vedic Reader for Students

The Upanishads, Part I of II

The Hymns of the Atharvaveda, Vol. 2 of 2

Read or order online at:

www.forgottenbooks.org
or
www.amazon.com